This book is dedicated to you, the reader in hope that

you and yours may be similarly transformed.

DIVINE ORDER
A Black Family's Transformation Through Organ Transplant

Kay T. Payne

Copyright © 2015 Kay T. Payne
All rights reserved.

ISBN: 1517213258
ISBN 13: 9781517213251
Library of Congress Control Number: 2015916050
CreateSpace Independent Publishing Platform
North Charleston, South Carolina

Contents

Foreword · · · vii
Preface · · · xi
Family Matrix (Siblings) · · · xv
Cast of Characters · · · xvii
Revelation · · · 1
Fear and Trembling · · · 23
Strength to Strength · · · 58
Transformation · · · 70
Epilogue · · · 81

Foreword

The Mayo Clinic's Consumer Health Report estimates that more than 100,000 people in the United States are awaiting a kidney donation. Unfortunately, many will never receive the call indicating that their second chance at life has been found. This scenario is even more distressing for African Americans, given that chronic diseases such as diabetes and hypertension are major causes of kidney disease, and ultimately end-stage renal disease, wherein a transplant is required.

The National Kidney Foundation (April 2014) reports: *Due to higher rates of diabetes, high blood pressure, heart disease and obesity, African Americans have an increased risk of kidney failure.* Further, the report indicates: *African Americans, while 13% of the overall population, constitute more than 32% of patients receiving dialysis. Diabetes is the leading cause of kidney failure in African Americans, who are twice as likely to be diagnosed with diabetes as Caucasians. There are approximately 4.9 million African Americans living with either diagnosed or undiagnosed diabetes. Among African Americans, high blood pressure is the second leading cause of kidney failure and is a leading cause of death.*

One does not need to search far to determine why transplantation is critically important to the individuals and families impacted by kidney disease. Without a functioning kidney, individuals have prognoses of decreased quality of life, long hours of renal dialysis, a high probability of other system failures, and death. Currently, more than one-third of all individuals waiting for a kidney donation are African American. Dr. Dorry Segev of Johns Hopkins University, investigator of a landmark study on African American kidney donation, reports that African Americans are least likely to receive a donation from a living donor.

Dr. Clive Callender, noted transplant surgeon and professor at Howard University School of Medicine, identified important actions that the African American community must take to reverse this distressing state of affairs. Major steps include becoming informed about the chronic conditions resulting in kidney disease, identifying family risk factors, and making necessary lifestyle changes where appropriate. Dr. Callender is founder of National Minority Donor Awareness Day, held annually in August. He is also a founding contributor to the National Minority Organ Tissue Transplant Education Program (MOTTEP), whose mission, based on the motto "Knowledge Empowers," is dedicated to the dissemination of accurate information to the African American community. In a research investigation on the reason African Americans do not participate in organ donation or identify themselves as organ donors (living or after death), Dr. Callender identified five misconceptions that affect the decision.

- *Organ donation is an unacceptable religious practice.* Dr. Callender responds, "When your spirit has departed this shell, there will be no organ count to ensure that everything is in place before you enter Heaven." In fact, he insists, "Organ donation is an act of love and the gift of life. After all, God gave His only son to ensure mankind the right to everlasting life."
- *Mistrust of the health care system including fear that identifying oneself as a donor would result in poor care (even a quickened death) if a crisis occurred requiring hospitalization.* This is absolutely untrue, as health facilities are sworn to provide required care to save and preserve life of all patients regardless of donor status.
- *Fear of being used as a research specimen and not receiving adequate care.* This statement is also a misconception, as all research requires the informed consent of participants.
- *Racism and covert practices (e.g., organs of an African American are given to white patients).* In fact, statistics indicate the inverse.

A disproportionate number of transplant recipients are African American, while most donors are white.
- *Inability to live a healthy, active life without one kidney.* Many people are born with only one kidney and live very active and happy lives unaware of this fact. Further, when one kidney must be removed due to trauma or infectious disease, patients do very well and live long lives, unaffected by the loss of one kidney.

There are other real-life issues that prevent African Americans from participating in organ donation. These include, but are not limited to, personal health status, inability to take off time from work, misinformation about hospital costs and insurance coverage, and fears related to altered body image or function.

As I prepare to conclude this Foreword, I would like for you, the reader, to take away two things. First, equip yourself with knowledge by knowing your numbers (blood pressure, total cholesterol, LDL, and HDL). This is accomplished by talking with your physician. Monitor changes in your general health (excessive fatigue; irritability; difference in the color of your urine; and puffiness or swelling in the ankles, hands, or eyes). Know the results of your lab work, and remember that the earliest sign of kidney trouble is protein in the urine. If this should occur, intervention is necessary. Don't delay and "watch it for a while."

The second and closing point is the challenge to create and identify an opportunity for transformation in your life, or the life of another, by a selfless act of kindness that can enhance or restore life. The author of *Divine Order*, by chronicling the events of her life and the experiences of her family, will impact the lives of many who are trapped by fear. Hearing about the personal stories of others is important because it is real and credible. Most important is the victory that comes from trusting and believing in God. I learned from the author that God, without my knowing as I hosted a television program featuring Dr. Clive Callender, used my life to provide a divine revelation to her. As a result, I am declaring it a blessing to be a part of the divine order and to contribute to the peace ordained for her family.

Many of you are members of African American families, have friends who are African American, and possibly know someone who is directly or indirectly affected by kidney disease. Remember that every ten minutes, another name is added to the waiting list. Most of these individuals will never live to receive the transplant they seek, particularly if he or she is African American. Organ donation is a real "gift of life." If you would like to become a donor, there are four ways to do so:

1. First, tell your family so they are aware of your wishes.
2. Designate your choice to be a donor on your driver's license.
3. Sign and carry a donor card.
4. Register with your state's donor registry.

Thank you for this opportunity to shine this light on life, love, and selfless giving.

Connie M. Webster, PhD, RN

Dr. Connie Webster is nurse researcher, professor of nursing and associate provost for academic programs at the University of the District of Columbia. Her research activities focus on elimination of health disparities and access to health care for African Americans. She is host of the cable television program Health Matters. *Watch the episode on kidney disease and transplantation that inspired* Divine Order *at* **www.youtube.com/watch?v=l9ISd0eYmdM.**

Preface

order *noun* (1): a command (2) systematic arrangement of events, people, or things (3): community under religious ministry (4): state of peaceful harmonious coexistence. *verb* (1): issue a directive (2): straighten, align (3): submit a request.

Near to completion of this manuscript, I still had no title for the epic that was being composed. I knew I desired to chronicle the events and emotions surrounding the decision to become a living kidney donor; the preparation, surgery, recovery and their ultimate meaning in a manner that would inform and inspire others to consider organ donation, particularly African Americans.

More than a year after surgery, in silent reverie in my favorite easy chair enjoying the warmth of a morning cup of joe, it occurred to me that the transplant not only involved my sister Carol and me, but it affected the entire family in the context of our African American heritage and devout prayer life. I realized that the decision to donate was not my personal determination. Rather, it was a divine command in answer to prayer. The events of our lives had been predestined and directed for this occasion, and moreover, the powerful, awesome hand of God was evident in each step on the path.

Hence the title *Divine Order* seemed appropriate. In the pages of this book you will come to know that because of prayer, our family unit was an *order* in Christian ministry. In prayer, we placed an *order* for Carol's miraculous healing from renal failure. Through the *order* of personal experiences, once my life was in *order*, in divine *order*, I received an *order* to donate a kidney. In *order* to effect the outcome, God assembled the players and events of the occasion in sequential and temporal *order*. In the outcome, as a family *order*, we now experience life in peaceful *order*.

The transplant was no in-out operation (pun intended). There were starts and stalls; upsurges and downswings; trepidations and occasional fears, doubts, and hesitations, but never a moment of dread or regret. In the end there was ultimate triumph. It is my wish to communicate through this volume that joy and divine favor come from obedience to God's command and trust in God's promise. Organ donation is perhaps one channel through which one can achieve peace and God's favor.

Penned during the year following the transplant, *Divine Order* recounts four stages of the donation process and accompanying sentiments through a series of episodes labeled "Revelation," "Fear and Trembling," "Strength to Strength," and "Transformation." "Revelation" describes the events of the divine call and acceptance as they were lived season by season up to the transplant surgery. Two personal meditations on courage and fortitude expound upon the events that led to the revelation.

"Fear and Trembling" provides a day-by-day account of each unsettling moment of the hospital experience, which leads the reader to vicariously appreciate the divine promise that ultimately prevailed. Moments of tension are eased by a sprinkle of wit, humor, or sarcasm. The chapter is followed by the single meditation "Giving, Forgiving, and Thanksgiving." The chapter "Strength to Strength" is evidence that joy comes in the morning. Through this chapter, *Divine Order* instructs its readers through elucidation of the character traits, practices, and support systems that led to the divine revelation and that undergirded the victory. Naturally, the meditations focus on prayer, family, and self-determination.

The final chapter, "Transformation," is itself a meditation. It is a philosophical treatise and reflection that details the ways in which our family was permanently uplifted by the transplant. It relates and gives meaning to the occurrences and brings closure in a manner that invites and encourages the reader to consider organ donation.

Divine Order is aptly titled because God ordered each step in the transplant process. Although its subtitle, *A Black Family's Transformation Through Organ Transplant*, might suggest a limited audience, the anecdotes of *Divine Order* can have broad social and demographic appeal. Indeed, organ transplant is a human event.

However, it is hoped that African Americans will particularly benefit from its message, inasmuch as organ donation is not a common practice. Some are reluctant to donate organs because of culture, tradition, and unsubstantiated beliefs associated with religion. Through the vehicle of an African American family, *Divine Order* shatters the mold of these beliefs and portrays the divine intervention dispatched.

In actuality, there are no precepts prohibiting organ donation for most religions. Unlike the Ancient Egyptians, who removed internal organs before mummification, the early Catholic Church prohibited such desecration of human remains, as it was seen as blasphemy. Indeed, Leonardo da Vinci contributed much to our current knowledge of anatomy through his illegal dissection of cadavers.

Inculcated from generational superstitions, some African Americans believe the body's internal workings plus one's ultimate fate are predetermined, and any attempt to alter these with modern scientific inventions, with the exception of healing practices, is to defy theology and mock God. Therefore, it is unthinkable to them to willfully disrupt the divine state of creation by removing organs, either during life or after death. In contrast, *Divine Order* demonstrates that, indeed, God occasionally wills the alteration of God's creation, and obedience to God results in divine favor.

Divine Order is written from the author's African American cultural perspective. There is no doubt the experiences of its characters are lived in the racial context of 21st-century America. In this regard, the book offers insight into the African American life experience and cultural existence.

It was the original intent to construct the book as a family venture in two parts so readers could receive perspectives of the donor and recipient together. Instead, two volumes were composed, including the forthcoming sequel, *Divine Providence*, which is the memoir of Carol, the kidney recipient.

It is said that the one who blesses is abundantly blessed, and those who help are helped. Of course, no great work is ever accomplished in isolation. Therefore, I must acknowledge all those who made this work possible. First in honor and glory to God, there would be no book without the divine inspiration to be a donor, as well as the vision to relate the experience as an inspiration others. To my sister, Carol, who shared the transplant experience as well as her thoughts in numerous conversations as we reflected on its meaning in our lives.

Professors can do little without the help of graduate assistants. Therefore, I must acknowledge Elan, who typed the manuscript and critiqued the content. Also gratitude is extended to Shameka, who acted as my reader and sounding board for the ideas and concepts; to my good friend Paula, who knows my mind; and to Sonja, who allowed me to bend her ear reading the draft as we sat far too long in restaurants.

Ultimately, I must recognize Elijah, my beloved, plus every member of my family for their loving support throughout the operation, as well as throughout the writing of this book. You allowed me to use your life experiences to enrich my own.

Family Matrix (Siblings)

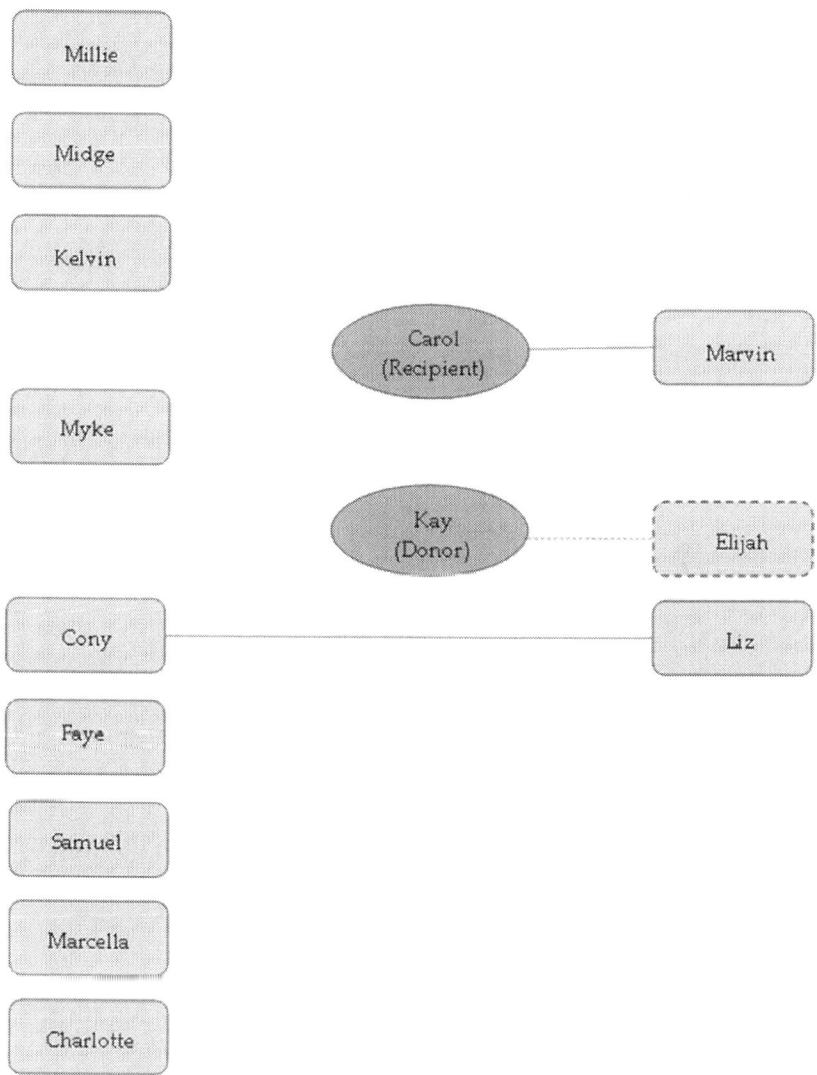

Cast of Characters

Kay: kidney donor, communications professor

Carol: kidney recipient, community service administrator

Charlotte: youngest of siblings, physician assistant, temporary caregiver to Kay

Marcella: singer, musician, and massage therapist; caregiver to Carol

Marvin: spouse and constant caregiver to Carol

Elijah: life partner of Kay, psychologist and administrator

Mary: longtime close girlfriend of Kay

Cony: retired law enforcement officer, deacon

Millie: eldest of siblings, retired flight attendant, hospital hospitality volunteer

Midge: elder sister, hospice social worker, temporary caregiver for Carol

Kelvin: "Bro," elder brother, one of the oldest living individuals with cerebral palsy

Liz: spouse of Cony, early childhood care provider

Revelation

The human body is fearfully and wonderfully made. We are endowed with two ears for localized hearing, two legs for vertical walking, and two hands for manual dexterity. If one is injured, our functioning is less than perfect.

Many organs such as the heart exist singularly to perform a specific vital function. But other essential organs exist in a matching set, serving a duplicate purpose. The kidneys are one such anatomical redundancy. God endowed humans with two kidneys so one could be willingly given to another person. And through this act of generosity, ironically, the giver is divinely perfected.

The biblical notion of *perfection* is translated from the Greek *telos*, which denotes fulfillment of the promise for which one was created. There is perhaps no greater act of perfection than organ donation. This is my testimony of how I came to be a living kidney donor—a sobering experience. My life and the lives of my family members were exceedingly uplifted as we came to realize that we were each specifically created and, through the evolution of our shared histories, predestined for this divine purpose.

From grade school through my doctoral study, the greater part of my life was spent in the academic environment. It was not that becoming a professor was fulfillment of a lifelong dream. This, much like every other aspect of my life, was fortuitous.

I admire people who control their destiny. I am quite the opposite. I only know that I don't care much for the ordinary. Multitalented from birth, I was extraordinary in high school. But in an exclusive, elite Upstate New York women's college, I was another fish in an ocean of extraordinary people. My creative energies were directed toward keeping ahead of the academic demands. African American students integrated into predominantly white institutions felt the need to prove we were equally as intelligent and capable. So failure was not an option. It would result in embarrassment and shame and reflect negatively on the entire race. So in college I focused on my studies, joined movements for social equality, and trained in nonviolent civil resistance in order to improve the lives of those who were not as fortunate as me.

After college, I was consistently in the winners' circle but was never the one who took home the prize. Often one of the top two candidates, I was the one who didn't get the job. Someone else had the right complexion, the competitive edge, or the inside connection. I detested playing second fiddle, but this seemed to mark the pattern of my existence. Success did not come easily. It came with immense struggle. I paid for every accomplishment with toil, sweat, and tears.

Always adventurous and prone to ramble, in later life as a professor, I discovered a way to be distinguished again. I determined to travel the world. In academia there were numerous opportunities ripe for the picking. And being single with a totally flexible work schedule, having no personal encumbrances, I possessed the requisite lifestyle. From the Middle East to the South Pacific, I proceeded from one journey to the next, ecstatic at being extraordinary again.

I love extended excursions to exotic places. Faculty excursions led me, much like Indiana Jones, to lands that other people had only read about in books or saw in movies. The excursions afforded the protection, comfort, learning opportunities, and all the amazing experiences imaginable. Each new adventure was a life-altering experience. I grew in knowledge, depth, wisdom, faith, and awe of the beauty of the earth and the modern and ancient worlds.

In retrospect, I suppose I was striving for new heights in order to escape an ordinary existence. Because after traveling to each exotic location, I would return to the humdrum of daily life, longing only to begin a new adventure. But one Sunday evening, little could I fathom the ultimate journey upon which I was about to embark—one that required no reservation or government-issued passport, and the adventure would last for the rest of my life.

Spring

In our family, the fourth Sunday of every month is a day for social gathering, a home-cooked meal, and prayer. I had returned from a tour of Spain and Morocco. The historical nuances of Spain provided context to the realities of the Western world. Much like it was in my favorite old movie, *Casablanca*, Morocco was a fascinating paradox. With the memories tucked safely in a photo album, I was set for an uneventful conclusion to the summer.

The stifling Washington, DC, weather had arrived. Women exchanged long-sleeve blouses for the cooling comfort of billowy sheers and sleeveless tank tops. I was aghast at the sight, through my sister Carol's dressy Sunday ensemble, of hideous scars on her arm. It appeared as though a small animal had been burrowing under her smooth mocha skin. With end-stage renal failure due to diabetes and high blood pressure, six months ago she had begun dialysis three days a week. Carol described how she endured the intense pain by calling upon angels for assistance. Worn out and exasperated, she had already initiated the process of joining the national kidney transplant waiting list.

I have always been squeamish about medical procedures, avoiding them as often as possible. I faint at the sight of blood, and the mere image of a needle renders me weak in the knees. I quickly turn away to avoid the assault on my serenity. As Carol described her experiences, I could vicariously sense her pain. Sensitive but feeling utterly helpless, I hadn't a notion there was anything I could do to assist.

That evening, the family prayed for miraculous recovery for Carol. We subconsciously hoped God would reverse the kidney failure. We always prayed that the family would receive a bounty of blessings and be readied for the windfall. In our minds, we yearned to strike it rich in the lottery. We believed that, through the strength of our faith, God would deliver. But such is the substance of dreams, not theology. God is not Santa Claus. We are not here to live our lives manipulating and controlling God by asking for earthly desires. If we are to experience the manifestation of our prayer requests, we must surrender ego control so God can transform our lives to make it so. But first we must prove ourselves worthy of the blessing and be willing to accept our role in making it possible.

Soon after the family departed, I began the arduous process of tidying up. Later I settled into the comfort of bed to rest and catch up on the latest news. Surfing the channels, I chanced upon the local University of the District of Columbia cable station. Featured was Dr. Connie Webster, host of *Health Matters*, with her guest and my colleague Dr. Clive Callender, an eminent African American kidney transplant specialist.

The discussion of kidney transplants was informative and compelling. My interest was particularly piqued since before being assigned to dialysis, which she believed was quite unnecessary, Carol asked me to research the alternatives. A friend and colleague, Dr. Bob Taylor, dean of a local medical school, explained that transplant was the most viable option. Instinctively, I assumed a living donor would be necessary. I inquired about the effect on a donor, especially their mental health should the transplant be ineffective. As physicians are loath to conjecturing, Bob was typically reserved. But he wholeheartedly supported the notion of transplant and provided a referral for a noted local nephrologist.

From *Health Matters*, I learned that the transplant waiting list is more than 101,000 strong. African Americans comprise the bulk of the recipients but only about 10 percent of the donors. Transplant survival and longevity are much improved for patients who receive a kidney from a live donor. Yet African Americans are the least likely to be living donors or to receive a kidney from a live donor. The wait for a transplant ranges from three to five years, and many patients die before a suitable donor is identified. After five years without a transplant, the survival rate for patients over age sixty-five decreases to 30 percent. I further learned that, since the kidney does not decline with advancing age, donors can range from newborn to sixty-five years and more. I was most enlightened to learn that there are no medical fees or health risks for a donor, and health insurance is not a requisite. The cost of the transplant is covered by Medicare or the recipient's health insurance.

There in my bed, something extraordinary touched me. In my personal prayer life, before rising I greet each day with meditation and conversation with God. I implore God to use me as his instrument of divine will. In this awesome moment, my prayer was answered as I received the revelation that I was to be Carol's kidney donor.

This was not my first encounter with the notion of kidney donation. Almost twenty years earlier, at a Sunday church event, youth minister Barry collapsed in what appeared to be a seizure. I used my limited knowledge of first aid to assist in his care. As we rode the half-mile in the ambulance to the hospital, his blood pressure spiked to dangerous levels. Hours later, presuming he was stabilized, I surrendered Barry to the expert hands of the physicians, expecting that he would rest one night and be released. The next day, after attempts to phone Barry failed, I discovered that he had been admitted to the ICU in respiratory failure. Barry was placed on a ventilator. Both kidneys had failed. This was unfathomable! Barry was a young man, not even forty.

In those days, securing a compatible donor was a more onerous process. With no willing family member as a match, Barry would bravely endure dialysis for several years. I don't remember how I learned that finally Barry was to have a kidney transplant. But I recall being profoundly impressed that a young woman in his congregation voluntarily stepped forward to be the donor. She conveyed that she was instructed by the Holy Spirit in a divine calling. For a Christian, a divine calling signifies a relentless summon to a holy endeavor from which there is no escape. There is agony in resistance and an ultimate reward in acceptance.

I longed for the type of relationship that young kidney donor had with God. At that time, I wondered why God had not lain such a calling on my heart. I hadn't given a single thought to kidneys until that warm Sunday evening in June. Indeed, when I was growing up, Mom told us that her sister in-law Ruth had lost one kidney. In her youth, someone had bested Aunt Ruth in a speakeasy brawl. From what we could tell, there were no ill effects on Aunt Ruth's life.

Summer

With the decision sealed, I kept silent until it was confirmed that Carol was on the transplant waiting list. During July's family prayer gathering at my home, over dessert, Carol confirmed she was on the list. To be declared an appropriate candidate, she needed to be physically able to withstand the operation, mentally heathy, and able to comply with a strict medicinal regimen for life. The prospect of having a living donor had not entered her thoughts. Instead, the family was hopeful that some benevolent, though unfortunate, soul would be her salvation.

As I leaned back in my favorite oversized easy chair, I found this to be an opportune moment to announce that I would be Carol's donor. Carol reacted first with astonishment, a long pause of disbelief, then tears of joy. Her expression first appeared as confusion that slowly melted to humility.

The men of the family, except Carol's husband Marvin, who was all verklempt, sat motionless, mouths agape, gazing wide-eyed in utter shock. The minute seemed to pass in slow motion as they pondered whether it would be a good idea or a terrible mistake, half-hoping I would proclaim it all a big joke.

The tension was broken as Charlotte immediately sprang into her professional role. As a physician's assistant, Charlotte is extremely knowledgeable. She had enjoyed a career on a surgical team until it was cut short by a reckless driver who rear-ended her car one rainy night while she was stopped at a traffic signal. She required surgery of her own to meld the cervical bones of her spine. The procedure left her with diminished sensory and motor function in her hands, which put an end to her surgical career.

Having taken an elective course in transplants in her academic program, she described the matching and presurgical preparation, which would entail lots of medical exams including a psychological evaluation for me. She further described the surgical procedure—two to three days in the hospital for me, and up to one month for Carol. There would be two surgical teams. Carol would emerge with three kidneys. Each of us would require caregivers. Being the most helpful, Marcella was the logical appointee for Carol. Since I would need an attendant following surgery, Charlotte rose to the task. We harbored not a doubt this was divine order and the answer to our family's prayer.

Naturally, I expected to be deemed suitable as a donor. I was in great physical shape. In the previous year I had reached a milestone birthday and devised a bucket list that included adopting a fitness routine. I engaged a fitness trainer, consumed a healthy diet, practiced yoga, jogged, and participated in the Avon Breast Cancer Walk. A previous surgery precluded fear of the unknown. Twenty years earlier, I had undergone major abdominal surgery. My first medical procedure, I feared I would not survive the procedure since, for the first time, I could not envisage the future. Instead, a cinderblock wall blocked the vista of life. Only pastoral counseling would bring me to the reality that God would not abandon me and everything would be alright. Ironically, I almost didn't survive. I hemorrhaged in surgery and the doctors had to take heroic action. But the recovery was complete and swift, and my health and the quality of my ensuing years were greatly improved.

During the subsequent week after prayer Sunday, Carol consulted her dialysis counselor to put the wheels in motion for the transplant. We are fortunate to live in the Washington, DC, area among top hospitals and one of the foremost transplant centers in the nation, Georgetown University Medical Center. I contacted the living donor coordinator, Christine Zutermeister, who explained that the entire process could take up to six months. Over the next month, the process proceeded like clockwork as I completed health surveys, read literature, viewed an information video, and scheduled the orientation. The summer was anything but uneventful.

During the presurgery orientation, I met my transplant team, which was headed by nephrectomy specialist Dr. Jennifer Verbesey. As she looked me directly in the eyes, immediately I trusted her implicitly and wanted her as my surgeon.

Trust is crucial when one is about to relinquish conscious control to general anesthesia. I know that many African Americans prefer a black doctor. When we finally relinquish home remedies, superstitious beliefs, and nontraditional medicine, African Americans prefer a physician with whom they can connect, one who acknowledges their intelligence, respects them as individuals, and truly values the importance of their lives. African Americans demand a physician's compassion as much as academic credentials, skill, precision, and accuracy.

These attributes, or lack thereof, are communicated in the physician's bedside manner. In Dr. Verbesey I knew I had found the full spectrum. From her gentle handshake I saw that Dr. Verbesey had delicate, healing hands. I knew that as women, there would be an emotional connection between us. If we had met under different circumstances, we would have been great friends. Her Caucasian racial heritage was of no consequence. And above all, her hands were the perfect size if they were to invade my delicate, slender frame.

At the Transplant Center, the waiting room was dominated by African Americans. During the orientation, I was pleased to be among two married donor-recipient pairs including one young African American couple. Because they were reticent to ask questions, I dominated the floor with my prepared list. How often is the donor monitored after surgery? What do the follow-up visits entail? What will happen if the donor develops kidney disease after the donation? Will I have any health concerns due to the absence of a kidney? Will I have to change my diet? Can I eat food from outside in the hospital? Will Carol and I share a room? To my delight, every question was addressed to my satisfaction. There would be no side effects, and there was a plan for every possible contingency. It was comforting to learn that as a donor, should I ever need a transplant, I would be advanced to the top of the transplant waiting list.

After consulting with various professionals, I expected more from the psychological evaluation. I imagined an in-depth analysis of my mental state with something akin to the old Rorschach inkblot test I had used as a psychology major. Basically the purpose of the consultation was to gain a sense of my emotional stability, fear, or hesitation, and to ascertain that I was not being coerced or selling my kidney for a profit. I guess I passed the test, but the psychologist must have been intrigued by my lack of emotion or concern. I can only imagine the guilt or regret that a donor might feel to realize they had given away a vital organ that could never be retrieved if their organ was rejected or if the recipient died. I had none of these fears because I believed God, like the birds of the air and the lilies of the field, would take care of me. Confident that I was of reasonably sound mind, the psychological evaluation consisted of a brief interview of about ten minutes. The psychologist indicated that he would be available if I should need counseling at any time, even after the transplant.

In fact, I had no misgivings about the procedure. However, I was appalled to learn that a donor can back down at any time and the transplant team will concoct a false reason to spare the recipient anguish. For example, I could abruptly change my mind at any time and Carol would be told that I was disqualified for some technical reason.

In retrospect I realized I had heard of such a potential case. An acquaintance was scheduled to receive a transplant from her son. Curiously, the surgery was suddenly postponed and never rescheduled. In such cases, psychological counseling would be available to spare the donor feelings of guilt. But I could never have dreamt of reversing the decision, dousing Carol's hope and devastating her life. Moreover, I would not want to spend my days living a lie with full knowledge that I was a coward while my sister might not witness the turn of another decade. And if she were to die of kidney failure, how could I look at myself in the mirror? I had never considered such emotions until they were ignited there in the presence of the psychologist.

Since type 2 diabetes is in our family genes, I had to be declared physically able to live with one kidney. That summer, it seems I took every medical test in the universe. A recent mammogram and colonoscopy were essential. I was required to submit a twenty-four-hour urine sample. How perfectly dignified to walk down the street swinging a gallon jug of urine! At least a dozen vials of blood and a glucose tolerance test were to follow. After drinking ultra-sweet syrup and waiting almost two hours, I was feeling quite faint, so I had to take the second set of needles lying down. That was all I could endure in a single trial. I rescheduled the echocardiogram and MRI for another day.

The echocardiogram was a stress test in which I walked a treadmill with advancing speed and gradual inclination. Because of fitness training, I passed with excellence, having the heart performance of a twenty-three-year-old. Take that, you millennials!

The MRI was the worst experience. Hooked to an intravenous tube and encased in a giant metal cylinder in a full-body stretch for forty-five minutes, the only save was the handsome, intelligent fortysomething technician who flattered me with playful flirtation. (At this age, I welcome all the flirtation I can get). Completely drained from the experience, I was compelled to take the long route home in an effort to calm my rattled nerves.

My risk of diabetes was negligible, and naturally Carol and I were found to be a perfect match. Donors and recipients are matched on the basis of six antigens within the blood to determine the probability of the recipient's immune system attacking the donated kidney. Modern science has advanced to a point that immunosuppressant drugs greatly reduce the probability of rejection. So a match on all six factors is not mandatory, but with a better match, the drug regimen can be less demanding and the life expectancy of the recipient greatly improved.

To be honest, in the wake of all the medical tests, I was already yearning for this adventure to conclude. I was ready to end the angst created by anticipation and experience the satisfaction of the aftermath. Surgery was set for October 15, and I felt fully prepared. I received nothing but esteem and support from friends and relatives. If anyone had a doubt or hesitation, they did not express it, not that any intervention to dissuade me would have met with success.

Elijah, my anchor and my beloved, was most supportive and encouraging. Venturesome and a restless wayfarer himself, he supported, without hesitation, every kooky idea that popped into my head. He enjoyed the tales of my travels as he vicariously experienced the adventures. Elijah has never advised me against following my dreams but stands patiently ready to catch me should I fall. That summer, we spent my birthday at the Washington Harbor while he pampered and lavished me with adoration and gifts.

As summer progressed, I began to train more vigorously and eat even more healthfully. Friends attest that I love my spirits. A nice crystal goblet of White Zinfandel with dinner helps me unwind after a long workday. In addition, nothing goes better, at the ballpark, with barbecue ribs, or Maryland blue crabs, than a tall, frosty Corona with a lime and a one-inch head. Nonetheless, I easily discontinued consumption and began to drink pure water. Since the abstention was for a good cause, I didn't miss the spirits.

Autumn

There was so much to do around the house before surgery. Surely I needed everything in order since following surgery I would not be able to do any lifting for a while. Besides, no one feels like doing physical work of any kind during recovery.

I was in a quandary about what to tell colleagues and church members. My friend Mary had been briefly hospitalized and was comforted by the attention from the score of church members who visited. Unlike Mary, I jealously guard my privacy and prefer to bear my tribulations in solitude. Moreover, it's good that I'm rarely sick because I'm very bad company. I don't mind people's prayers from a distance, but I didn't want to have to explain the details or relate the story over and over. So I decided to confide in a small circle of colleagues, friends, and church members.

Surgery postponed! It hit like a sucker punch in the dark. The phone rang around two o'clock the afternoon before surgery day. It turned out that Carol needed to apply for insurance coverage for the lifetime of medications she would require. Even though they are a bargain compared to dialysis, the expense is more than all except the wealthy can afford without insurance.

The postponement threw me for a whopping loop. The feeling of disappointment was something I could not have imagined. I can empathize with women who have had a miscarriage. I was supposed to birth a miracle, but it didn't happen. In addition, since the decision to donate was extremely delicate, I could not guarantee that I would have the same sentiment when the surgery was rescheduled.

I had arranged a month of medical leave, but on the day surgery was to have occurred, I was forced to return to work as usual. Life was surreal, like an existential drama in which I was present but not in the cast. I was actually experiencing life as it would have been without my presence. My colleague, Connie, listened patiently and gifted me with a lovely journal and a warm embrace.

Surely, the delay delivered a blow to Carol as well. She had joyously celebrated her final appointment with the dialysis center staff. There is probably no word for the emotion she must have felt as she had to return to dialysis the next day.

The Transplant Center indicated that it would take at least forty-five days before the new insurance could be processed and surgery rescheduled. The date was tentatively set for December 4. At least that would present enough time for my recuperation during the holidays and semester break, and allow a full return to work for the second semester.

The holidays arrived and left. The fall foliage vanished and the autumn harvest décor gave way to festive yuletide decorations, a tree and lights. The family gathered on Christmas Eve as the young ones delighted in their gifts. Yet before Thanksgiving, I had grown suspicious that Carol was not vigorously pursuing the insurance. Although the Transplant Center recommended AARP Medicare supplemental insurance, Carol engaged a young *un*professional insurance broker to research a better option. It was during the time that millions of Americans were shopping for insurance under the Affordable Care Act, or Obamacare. To date, that broker has never found a more suitable option, nor has he returned any of her numerous calls. I was incensed to learn this. What kind of individual would commit the unconscionable act of stalling a transplant patient?

In the meantime Carol had begun to listen to friends and hold out faith that her kidney function would be miraculously restored. But in reality, for end stage renal failure, kidney function is not reversible as in some infections and injuries. Only upon my insistence that if the surgery were not conducted during winter break it would have to wait until spring did Carol finally seize the initiative to terminate that insurance broker and apply for the AARP insurance as first recommended.

The delay was divine order. During the respite, I began to sort out my thoughts and emotions. Since everything happened so quickly after the decision to donate, Carol and I had never had a soul-to-soul talk. Nor had I undergone deep reflection on the matter. This is definitely uncharacteristic since I am usually the contemplative and analytical sort. With most other life decisions, by now I would have read several books, prayed, and perhaps fasted. I felt that if I paused to analyze the decision, I might overthink it and back down, letting fear triumph.

But this kidney donation was a divine revelation, not an intellectual decision. My faith instructs me that when God ordains something, it cannot fail. But intellectually, I know that human free will can temporarily obstruct God's purpose. That's why we align our actions with God's purpose in the Lord's Prayer when we implore, *"Thy will be done on earth as it is in heaven."*

While medicinal herbs and trees are cited in the Bible as sources of healing, I am a proponent of modern scientific medicine. Carol is the antithesis. With a penchant for mysticism, she studied nontraditional holistic, naturalistic, Ayurvedic, and homeopathic treatments and believed that a proper diet was the key to health and well-being. On the other hand, I maintain that these are great for prevention and health maintenance, but once disease is in progress pharmaceuticals work by altering the molecules within affected cells in a direct, immediate, and effective way that avoiding or stocking up on foods and herbal remedies cannot duplicate.

I suppose I contributed in a small way to Carol's mystical beliefs. In college, alone in a small Upstate New York township, I desired the cheerful companionship of my favorite sister. Carol had completed undergraduate study and was searching for an appropriate graduate school. Young, naïve, and reckless as we were, we consulted the Ouija board. Knowing Carol was gullible and suggestible, when she asked what university she would attend, I guilefully spelled out C-O-R-N-E-L-L because Cornell University was within an hour's drive from my campus. I enjoyed having my sister close by during those years but later felt guilty about manipulating her fate. Carol endured several heartbreaks and hardships during her years at Cornell.

I believe that it was her preference for nontraditional treatments that created Carol's present health situation. Eight years earlier, the family first witnessed Carol's incipient decline. At holiday gatherings, she lacked energy and slept excessively. The family observed a decrease in memory and cognition; and as her vision declined, she was a terror behind the wheel. She was diagnosed with "drop foot" and consigned to an assistive mobility device. Only after diagnosis of diabetic retinopathy did she accept that the problems were due to type 2 diabetes. Two years later, she relocated to rural Georgia for a brief span, where her condition further deteriorated. I will always believe that a plethora of pharmaceuticals, less than adequate health care, and nontraditional remedies led to kidney failure. Returning to Maryland, she was immediately assigned to dialysis.

Throughout dialysis, Carol continued nontraditional treatments. The more her condition declined, the more she relied on nontraditional treatments. She consumed an armful of different pills and vitamins regularly. Hence, I came to imagine that after the transplant, she would eventually abandon the required immunosuppressant medications. I reasoned that it was probably her disdain for traditional medicine that kept her from applying for the insurance. This was my only hesitation. These things I pondered and kept within my heart because if the Transplant Center knew, they might declare her unsuitable and cancel the procedure.

It is natural for a donor to fear their kidney might be rejected by the recipient's body, or the recipient might die, rendering the transplant for naught while leaving the donor absent their organ. Almost two years following her surgery, I met Chauntae. An African American graduate student in my sociolinguistics class, she sauntered into the office full of energy with bright eyes, bunny rabbit cheeks, and a sense of class and style beyond her meager years. Chauntae had received two kidney transplants. Her first, from a loyal friend as a living donor, had been rejected after several weeks. I cannot imagine the anguish the young man must have endured after the rejection of his kidney.

In my situation with Carol, certainly, the physiological ramifications were of concern, but there are also practical issues. It would be infuriating for me to learn that my precious organ was not being nurtured, or that Carol's original health condition similarly affected the donated kidney. These were considerations I had not previously contemplated, allowing faith to banish negative thoughts and compel me headstrong into what I believed was my preordained destiny. The same faith compelled me to stay the course in the wake of these thoughts.

Of course, the idea of a transplant can be daunting for the recipient as well. Although we didn't speak of them specifically, I imagine Carol had emotional hesitations of her own. In July we had jokingly discussed cell memory, which is the phenomenon wherein a transplant recipient mysteriously assumes a peculiarity or a connection to the donor. Carol lightheartedly exclaimed that through this bond she would finally get her doctorate. I retorted that, more likely, she would develop a strong desire for White Zinfandel. She chortled and said she could live with that. But I could sense that the prospect worried her.

I suspect that Carol's feelings were deeper than she cared to admit. Though she is a Believer in Christ, Carol also holds to non-Western religious tenets, especially the notion of karma. Karma is the ancient Sanskrit cosmic law of distributive justice. Good karma is earned by living righteously, and bad karma is retribution for unrighteous deeds.

But karma does not explain why bad things happen to good people, or why some bad people prosper. For that, one needs to understand God's grace and mercy and our redemption through Jesus Christ. God loves us equally, and we cannot earn extra love. And because of Christ's sacrifice for our sins, we all receive more grace and mercy than we deserve or could ever earn.

Yet, Carol would never want to assume the karma debt of another person. I admonished her that for the transplant waiting list, karma is not one of the matching criteria. Besides, one would do extremely well to get *my* karma. Nonetheless, Carol continued to pray for miraculous recovery. I finally made a breakthrough by reminding her that I was the vessel of her miracle—her Godsend—the answer to our family's prayer, and by having a perfectly matched living donor, she had indeed hit the transplant lottery with a prize more valuable than all the riches of the universe!

Winter

Alas, surgery was rescheduled for Tuesday, February 4. I had about three weeks to once again prepare for recovery. I was relieved that an end was finally in sight. Due to the time lapse, both Carol and I were required to undergo another round of presurgical tests. This meant another dozen blood vials, but not the strenuous physical protocols. As one of her therapeutic specialties, Marcella offered me her special ion detox foot spa, which is alleged to remove impurities from the body through a soothing foot soak. Scientific or psychological, afterward I felt more vibrant.

I envisioned a three- to four-week recovery. So I planned to reward myself while simultaneously setting a goal to aspire toward during recuperation. For the third week of recovery, I would enjoy a rest and recovery vacation cruise at sea where I would lie on deck, have full luxurious meals, and do as much or as little as I pleased. Plus, I would be cruising to a warm climate with sunshine and flowers, which always make me happy in winter. I did not worry about the need for onboard medical assistance. Although I have no qualms about traveling alone, I wanted a roommate not only because the cheap winter fares were for double occupancy, but of course, because it is wise to have a companion to share the fun. But there were few who could afford the luxury of basking in the sun for a full week. Being retired and available, my friend Mary had expressed interest in October, but I did not know whether the offer was still on the table.

Months ago, I had prepared the house for my recuperation. Although I have no proclivity for housekeeping, I again purged the refrigerator of expired condiments, as well as the leftovers so old they had fuzzy gray beards. Colleagues readily offered to substitute in my classes. My graduate students, without knowing the exact nature of the leave of absence, were set to prove they could take up the mantle and carry on in my absence.

On the Sunday preceding surgery, the family gathered for dinner and prayer. No one hinted of fear or hesitation. Everyone was completely confident that all would go well. Each individual had accepted his or her role and was committed to its fulfillment. Yet we prayed for God's intervention in every aspect of the procedure.

There was little left to do but get primed emotionally. I treated myself to a luxurious spa replete with Jacuzzi, aroma therapy massage, facial, brow trim, manicure, and pedicure with vibrant happy colors. I opted for a sassy, head-turning haircut guaranteed to stop traffic or your money back. A chic fleecy Juicy Couture track suit remained in the hospital bag packed in October. Having pledged my organs, I was well aware of the risk of dying in surgery, and if this were to be my demise, I was going to check out looking good.

Although I could have easily called a driver to deliver me to the hospital, the night before surgery, Charlotte slept over to be my escort. I attended yoga class as usual. Meditation during the Shavasana yoga pose helped bring spiritual focus and relieve any leftover anxiety.

I had been instructed to cease all vitamins and medications one week before, and there was to be no eating or drinking after midnight—nothing to stimulate the gastric juices, including swallowing while brushing. A special antibacterial potion was prescribed to shower with before getting into a bed with freshly laundered linens and pajamas. Plus, there was to be another shower the next morning with fresh towels and the remainder of the potion. Check-in was scheduled for 5:30 a.m. Tuesday morning.

Courage

All my acquaintances said donating a kidney was a noble action. It is said that African Americans are reluctant donors. However, not one person questioned or challenged my decision or expressed surprise that I would be one to do it. Yet, none had ever personally known a donor, either deceased or living.

My decision was the result of divine revelation. I am known to be an independent and headstrong individual. Whatever I set my mind to do I generally see it through to the end. For example, with the decision to pursue divinity study, failure to go all the way to confirmation of the degree was never an alternative. That, too, was divine revelation.

In May several years before the transplant, I received exhilarating news that I was selected as a Fulbright fellow to Egypt. Naturally, as my life story would have it, my first choice was China. But who would look a gift horse in the mouth? I would find that voyage to Egypt to be a life-altering experience.

I knew very little about Mount Sinai except for what had been portrayed on the big screen in Cecil B. DeMille's 1956 blockbuster *The Ten Commandments*. That star-sprinkled summer night, the Fulbright group set out to arrive at the summit for the rising of the sun, as the Ancient Egyptians had done millennia before. It's good that it was dark as we embarked, because if I had seen what lay ahead, I probably would have lost the nerve.

Hours later and halfway up the trail, the air became thin as fatigue set in. I paused next to a knee-level stone wall dividing the precipice from the abyss below. Some pilgrims on the journey had paid Bedouin to deliver them up the trail by camel. As I hesitated briefly to catch a breath, a camel led by his master rounded the bend speeding toward his next passenger. That camel would come within inches of sideswiping and knocking me headfirst into the ravine without anyone ever knowing except the swarming buzzards that came to the feast. As I stared terrified into the eye of the wildly careening animal, in a flash I learned a lesson on the sure-footedness of a camel. Their quadrupled gait is enabled by multijointed hind legs. That night, I cheated death by the quick side-step of a dromedary. Whether it was the hand of God, or my guardian angel, I was too terrified and too weary to ponder.

Nearing the top of Mount Sinai as dawn was breaking, I could barely stand. Propped up by my young guide and giddily singing a medley of "Here comes the sun, do-do-do-do" and "Sun, sun, sun/ here it comes," my feet marched with a will of their own. There was little hope of making it to the summit. So I sought a respite on the plateau known as Elijah's Basin, the place where the Prophet Elijah was believed to have ascended to heaven in a chariot of fire.

A member of the Fulbright party, a spiritual African American young woman, was already descending. She explained that she sensed negative energy from the tourists there on the summit. Content, we sat together on Elijah's Basin while Bedouin supplied us with warm blankets and hot tea.

As dawn turned to day, my mind was dazed and my heart raced with awe. Its ritual for millions of years, the rising sun was magnificent to behold. It rose slowly to the horizon, then quickly into the beckoning sky as if someone had scooped an egg yolk from its bowl. The incredible peace at Elijah's Basin was nothing I had ever experienced. In keeping with a lifetime of playing second string, I realized that I was not meant to reach Mount Sinai's summit— because something touched my soul there on Elijah's Basin.

It is the American ideal to be the first, the best, and the foremost. There is no value and no appreciation for second place. What my Fulbright companion sensed on the summit of Mount Sinai symbolizes the corruption that often accompanies the race to the top and the struggle to remain there.

Following a brief stay, there was little time to tarry as we needed to descend the trail since the temperature in July quickly climbs to 120 degrees by 10:00 a.m. Breakfast awaited at the foot of the trail, but I had no desire for physical food. On the four-hour bus trip back to Sharm El Sheikh, everyone else slept from sheer exhaustion. But I sat wide-eyed and pensive with enough energy to run a marathon. I would not realize how my life was altered on Elijah's Basin until years later. However, in the years that followed, I began to devour books on religion and became enthralled with ancient history and all things celestial. I was led to enroll in a course in the Old Testament. From this overture, I would commit to getting a master's degree in religious studies at my university's school of divinity.

In the beginning, I could not imagine how I would be able to work full time and take courses. But miraculously, God awakened me at dawn to read the assignments. I had always considered myself a slow reader, but by some wonder, I read the textbooks twice as fast and with greater comprehension. When it came to writing, after earnest prayer, I felt as though it were something outside me that took hold of the pen. The thoughts, seemingly not my own, were much more profound than my typical musings.

The experience on Elijah's Basin led me to accept my designated place in life, second as it may be. It is not necessary to always make it to the top. God can reach us wherever we are if we open ourselves to divine will. Had I reached the summit, among the negative energy of the competitive world, I would have missed my blessing.

So once I received the revelation to donate a kidney, I already knew what it would feel like to complete the mission. Thus, I cannot say that it required courage. Courage is a personal source of determination summoned from within. It is a human choice without the assurance of a divine promise. By contrast, a divine revelation entails a discovery of the purpose of one's life within the context of God's promise. It begins with a righteous relationship with God. With a divine revelation, fear is vanquished; hence, courage is unnecessary. Upon receiving a revelation, one can release personal control and lose oneself in faith, full trust, and anticipation of the fulfillment of the divine promise.

Fortitude

People describe me as the Rock of Gibraltar. Actually, I've seen Gibraltar. As the tour bus rounded the bend on the highway to Algeciras, Spain, the image abruptly burst into sight like a light turned on in the dark. Gibraltar is an awesome colossal rock protruding from the waters at the mouth of the Mediterranean Sea. Skyscrapers embedded in the hillside appear as scaled architectural models. It is a stark reminder of how God is greater than creation. From the window of the Hotel Globales Reina Cristina, I watched as dusk fell and the lights of Gibraltar rose to speckle the velvet darkness and again as the brilliance of the new dawn bleached them away. Thanks for the compliment, but I am no Gibraltar.

Once in a radio contest, I won a set of albums. When I was a brooding teenager, my favorite rock song was Simon and Garfunkel's "I Am a Rock." The final verse goes "…and a rock feels no pain and an island never dies." How unfortunate to be an island made out of rock. I do not wish to be Gibraltar. I need to feel the loving comfort of fellow human beings as well as humility in the greatness of God. Praise to God, I am no longer that teenager with the sullen adolescent temperament. However, what remains today is tenacity. I'm often referred to as a woman of determination, and I like to think that's true.

Transporting back to youthful experiences, for the first five years of life, I was a thumb-sucker. I recall nights when Dad put Texas Pete hot sauce on my thumb to break me of the habit. But defiantly I would break the habit quite on my own, thank you. One fine day before the start of first grade, I decided to make a change. I determined that if I could resist the temptation to suck my thumb three times, I would be free. Like the three temptations of Christ—once for the Father, once for the Son, and once for the Holy Ghost—it's a law of the universe. The enemy will have to flee. This strategy has been working in my life ever since.

Once my mind is set on something, nothing can cause me to waiver. Mom characterized my willful ways as stubborn and contrary. But as long as they were channeled into good intentions, she never chastened me. Shortly after the thumb-sucking defeat, there was a doll contest in Miss Joyner's primary Sunday school class. I do not recall the exact prize, but to me the reward was the honor of achievement. The prize was to go to the little girl who looked the most like her doll. Being a talented seamstress, Mom had sewed my beautiful, crisp sundress complete with crinoline slip. From the cutaway scraps, she made the identical outfit for my doll. No one could top that, or so I believed.

I will never forget that momentous Sunday morning. As I sat perched in anxious anticipation, in strolled my archrival, *Va-Va*-Viveen, making a grand entrance down the center aisle bedecked in a bridal gown, complete with train and veil, while flaunting her look-alike bride doll. I was completely blown away! Again I took second place. But at the ripe age of six years old, I vowed that from that moment forward, no one would surpass me again. I discovered what is known as a winning attitude. Winning requires an effort that is over the top and miles ahead of the competition. One must expect that the competition will be ordinary, then win by being extraordinary. As a result of this thinking, I went through every grade with all of my classmates in my dust. How do you like me now, Viveen? Huh? (I hope she's not reading this.)

Tenacity accompanied me to adulthood. I discovered that, for the important concerns, prayer was always first in the order. I also honed the discipline of fasting. There is no better avenue to understanding God's purpose for one's life than fasting. Fasting is not to be confused with dieting. While dieting has its physical goal of losing weight, fasting is an earthly action undertaken to achieve a divine manifestation. Done in solitude along with sincere discipline, reflection, and meditation, fasting enables us to set aside mundane concerns and focus on God and to align our actions with God's purpose.

I cannot declare that all my prayers have come to fruition. Actually, there has been great wailing and gnashing of teeth. But through the failures of life, I learned that it's not what I desire but what God wants for my life. I learned to pray, asking not for earthly possessions but that the outcomes of my actions are in concert with my divine purpose. So my prayer is not for my will to be God's, but for God's will to be manifested in me.

I recall, as a young adult beginning a career, I prayed fervently for a particular job that I thought was ideal for my expertise and experience. Ironically, I did not receive so much as the dignity of a response from the employer. It was not until years later I recognized how that job would have changed the course of my life.

I love my life now. When I reflect on the totality of my existence, I recall a prayer written by an unknown civil war soldier.

> I asked God for strength, that I might achieve
> > I was made weak, that I might learn humbly to obey
>
> I asked for health, that I might do great things
> > I was given infirmity, that I might do better things
>
> I asked for riches, that I might be happy
> > I was given poverty, that I might be wise
>
> I asked for power, that I might receive the praise of men
> > I was given weakness, that I might feel the need of God
>
> I asked for all things, that I might enjoy life
> > I was given life, that I might enjoy all things
>
> I got nothing that I asked for; but everything I hoped for
> Almost despite myself, my unspoken prayers were answered
> I am, among all creatures, most richly blessed

I am a living demonstration that joy does not derive from reaching the top, acquisition of riches or power, material possessions, or the esteem of others. The real joy of life is being perfected in God's favor, and this is the true meaning of prosperity.

Fear and Trembling

Tuesday, Surgery Day

It had been an unusually harsh winter in the nation's capital. There were more snow days than I could recount in recent history. President Obama had branded us "weather wimps" because in Washington, the entire city infrastructure becomes paralyzed at the mere anticipation of a snowflake. I couldn't bear another postponement, so I designed a contingency. If it snowed the night before surgery, Carol and I would check into the Georgetown University Inn, a literal stone's throw from the hospital.

But alas, a cold crisp daybreak greeted the occasion. Little did I know it was the eye of the hurricane. Even the wind was solemn. The streetlights did little to pierce the bleakness of the predawn sky. My mood was somber, and like an automaton, I showered, dressed, and plodded toward the car. Forging ahead without emotion, I neither looked to the past to question the decision, nor ahead to envisage the aftermath.

I was on time for the 5:30 a.m. check-in without a glitch. The admitting area was newly renovated with pleasant furnishings and full of light. Dozing intermittently, Carol with husband Marvin had already arrived. I admired the effort it must have taken since Carol lived far from the hospital, and because of her limited mobility, everything required a monumental time investment. Surgery could not begin until the medical teams had witnessed the presence of both donor and recipient and ascertained that both were willing to move forward.

I had read about a botched surgery in which a freshly harvested kidney was dropped, rendering it contaminated and unusable. In another incident, the newly harvested kidney was accidentally discarded in the trash. Despite these images, I remained undaunted.

After a brief period in the waiting area as we watched the tropical fish in the aquarium swimming without a care in the world, Carol was called to the presurgical area first although her procedure was to begin about ninety minutes after mine. The plan was that while the acquisition team was detaching my left kidney, Carol would be prepared for transplantation of it into her lower abdomen. It was explained that my procedure would last about three hours while Carol's would last five hours. I imagined that it took a great deal of time to meticulously detach the kidney and reattach all the tissues, nerves, and blood vessels.

Once situated in the presurgical area, my surgical team arrived and introduced themselves, not that I would remember their names or faces. The anesthesiologist explained that I would receive a mild sedative in the presurgical area and then be wheeled into the surgery room and administered general anesthesia.

In the presurgical area, Carol and I were outfitted with faded, wrinkled hospital gowns that opened in the back and looked like they were sewn from old-fashioned feed sacks. We were stationed in our hospital beds parked in two areas separated by drawstring curtains. Family members were allowed to visit. Most of the attention, exhibited as loving concern, was focused on Carol. As Georgetown Medical Center is affiliated with the Jesuit order, prayer is considered a component of treatment. So, it was a special moment as the attendants wheeled my bed next to Carol's, and as we held hands, Cony offered a fervent prayer. That's the last thing I remember. The brain on anesthesia is a curious entity, and no one can be held accountable for what they might say. Charlotte reports that, in a very sassy tone, I told her to shut up. But I can't attest to that.

Hours later, with every system numb, and groggy from anesthesia, I was awakened and told that I was all done. To my mind, I had never left the presurgical area. The first thought was *I survived* followed by *So this is what it feels like to have one kidney.* There was no difference in the way I felt now from four hours before, except for tautness of the skin of my abdomen, a sense of completion, an unspeakable peace, and an unquenchable desire to sleep.

Through the corridors with which I had become so familiar from previous appointments, I was ushered to a private room on the surgical floor. A dismal gray pallor bathed the walls. Actually, I prefer a soft pastel green. Through the residual anesthesia I wondered, *Who picks hospital colors anyway? Don't they know soothing color and light are important for healing? These things uplift the spirit and unleash natural healing powers. Those guys probably never had surgery in their lives.*

The orderly positioned the bed so I had a full view of the corridor and the bustling activity therein. From the window opposite the bed, I could only peer into the office in the adjacent building; nonetheless, it afforded a source of natural light. Ironically, today the sun was overtaken by a blanket of winter clouds. From bed, I was comforted by the crucifix deliberately hung at the highest point of the wall so as to be observable from every vantage point. It was a focal point that beckoned me to meditate between dozes.

Earlier that morning in the waiting room, I had been assigned a patient number for loved ones to phone to check the progress of surgery and my recovery status. The service didn't work, causing frustration and leaving friends, especially Elijah, frantic for information. Fortunately, Charlotte was posting updates on Facebook for the family. But I had no concern for the outside world or the people in it.

The process of recovery begins immediately after surgery. The anesthesia had suppressed all bodily functions. In order to restore full lung capacity, I was issued a plastic spirometer, which measures air being sucked into the lungs through the mouth, and I was instructed to do this ten times each hour. The spirometer was a bother, so instead I practiced yoga deep breathing. Actually, there are many yoga movements that can be beneficial to post-surgical recovery. *I could patent my own brand of post-surgical restorative yoga.*

The young nurses were extremely attentive, as I probably wore out the call button. Uncomfortable with the intravenous tube, monitors, catheter, and compression stockings, I became nauseous on the initial attempt to sit erect. Nurses were quick to administer Atarax. Although, I sensed no pain, oxycodone was injected on schedule once an hour. This narcotic medication, together with the residual anesthesia induced sleep replete with inane dreams. *Some Central American immigrants had set up household in one of the parking spaces in the hospital garage.*

It would prove to be a restless sleep, dozing five minutes and awake again for ten, with nurses and technicians intruding each hour to administer antibiotics and monitor vital signs. To help with the sensation of dry mouth, my assignment was to drink two liters of water; and to protect the one precious kidney I had, I took the order very seriously. Restricted to a liquid diet, I hungered for some good food while waiting expectantly to receive word that Carol's surgery was complete.

Charlotte and I waited hours into the evening anticipating the report. Various family members and visitors arrived on a rotating schedule. The five o'clock news ended without a word. Lacking the presence of mind to pray, for the first time, I worried.

I now realize the importance of the hospital chaplain. When patients cannot pray themselves, they need someone to deliver a prayer on their behalf. Meek and soft-spoken with a thin plastic smile plastered on his face, the lanky, pale-faced Jesuit priest arrived and inquired if I desired prayer. On impulse I almost declined, silently protesting, "I'm Baptist," but I relented because his puppy dog eyes beseeched me. His muted, mumbled generic prayer, recited from memory, had nothing in the world to do with my predicament. What I needed at this moment was the fire and brimstone of a down-home black Baptist preacher to rain down blessings from the Heavens. A constant force in the hospital experience, that chaplain would become my mainstay. In the days to follow I welcomed his ebullient face and imploring eyes.

Carol would not be admitted to her room across the hall until twelve hours after the procedure. After 9:30 p.m., the visits ceased. Confident Carol was alright, I tried in vain to get some sleep. Lying in bed, I remembered Mom and Dad and felt assured that somewhere in eternity, their spirits were pleased.

Wednesday

February 5, the day after surgery, was twenty years to the day after Mom departed for the heavenly realm. She developed kidney stones in midlife and lived her remaining years with a portion of one kidney. In those days, the only treatment was complete or partial nephrectomy. Years later, Mom developed type 2 diabetes. In the end, this and high blood pressure resulted in months of physical distress. I had not given much thought to the possibility of a genetic tie to Mom's condition until Carol's troubles began.

On that day, twenty years earlier, exhausted from traveling and having medical complications, I flew to LaGuardia because doctors said that Mom was lingering and barely clinging to life. Weeks prior, Millie and I had consented to her wishes and signed a DNR, or "Do Not Resuscitate" order so Mom could pass peaceably to her reward.

I was the final sibling to arrive at the hospital. Mom, weak but conscious, immediately opened one eye as if to greet me. In the afternoon, Millie, Myke, and I headed to a nearby New York diner for lunch. Chic fashionistas and bargain hunters, on the return we couldn't resist a midwinter sale. Due to a lengthy checkout line, we did not arrive back to the hospital until early evening. Mom was propped up in a sitting position and resting peacefully. Myke lowered the bed so she could lie comfortably. Distracted, as we basked in the purchases to expressions of "Ooh," and "How much?" when we refocused attention on Mom, she had slipped away with the angels. I believe it was Mom's desire to exit quietly during a cheerful moment while the attention was not on her.

On the present February 5, the day after surgery, Washington awakened to a nasty ice storm. Schools were closed and the streets resembled a hockey rink. There were fender-benders galore and some people had flipped their cars upside down. So I expected no visitors and was perfectly content with that. I didn't want anyone to risk life or limb for my sake. Besides, the concerns of the outside world were far from my consciousness. The continual ringing of the phone drew me back to reality. Although I didn't relish the attention, I relented because loved ones needed to hear my voice to be assured I was alright.

Through my view of the corridor, just after dawn, I glimpsed a patient being wheeled off the surgical floor. From her arm, I recognized that it was Carol. This could not be a good thing. Asking the nurse, I was, as my students say, "HIPAA*ed*." HIPAA stands for the Health Insurance Portability and Accountability Act, which regulates strict confidentiality of patient health information. My quest for information met stern resistance, as I was dutifully instructed that I could contact Carol's next of kin. According to my logic, as sisters now sharing an internal organ, I *was* Carol's next of kin. I seethed with both rage and frustration.

Unsuccessfully, I strive to be a person of even temperament. I believe that anger is a self-injurious, unproductive waste of emotional energy. In anger, we allow disturbances of the environment to deprive us of better judgment. In anger reactions, self-righteous indignation renders us unable to connect with God. At times as this, I'm able to block out the world and retreat within. Today, as I was powerless to improve the situation, I gave it over to God, collected my faculties, and phoned Marvin. Though it was quite early, he was awake and energetic. He knew the situation but was completely unfazed. It seems that Carol had spent a difficult night. Her usually high blood pressure had plummeted, necessitating a move to the intensive care unit.

Later that morning, I was successful in wrenching information from the alert, handsome attending physician. He believed Carol had had a mild heart attack. "Wait! What?" Although his lips were moving, I heard nothing past *heart attack*. I wanted him to leave me alone so I could replay the tape of what I thought I had heard. Indisputably, this was a time when anyone would be within their rights to panic. Had the transplant nearly killed Carol? Was she too weak to endure the surgery? Maybe it would have been better to have left well enough alone. Would this have happened in October? Perhaps the transplant was not God's will after all. My emotions vacillated from terror to frustration, from worry to guilt.

Retreating to my inner sanctuary, I called upon faith. The thwarted expectation of what humans believe to be equitable and fair leads us to doubt God and God's providence. But faith recognizes that God's ways are not our ways and that God's purpose is achieved behind the scenes in historical outcomes, not in discrete worldly actions and events. To accomplish the former, God disperses angels.

Somehow, through all the emotional wrangling, it did not feel like tragedy. I had previously been acquainted with the feel of terror in losing Carol. It was the day of the fatal Metrorail collision. Carol's job at a local university required a commute from suburbia to the heart of the city. Hearing that the names of the deceased were being withheld until the families were notified, I felt the stab of a jagged-edge dagger piercing my innards. It was as if the sting of a scorpion radiated throughout my body until I heard Carol's animated voice on the telephone. But today, the sensation was not the same. I like to think there were angels present with me, providing comfort and assurance. There was to be no dying this February 5. I summarily dismissed the angels of doom.

Because I was still relegated to liquid sustenance, breakfast consisted of cranberry juice, a small bottle of Ensure, and 900 milliliters of water. After lunch, to my relief, the nurse removed the catheter and compression stockings. By noon I had lain in a hospital bed for nearly thirty hours, desperately wanting to sit upright in a chair. The room was insufferably hot. The nurse disengaged the heart monitor and intravenous tube and assisted me in the short walk to the lavatory as she prepared the visitor's chair with a fresh sheet and nice fluffy pillow.

As I emerged, pleased that my system was back in working condition, I began to feel light-headed. This was not an unfamiliar sensation. A similar episode had occurred the first time I stood after the surgery twenty years ago. Previously diagnosed with vaso-vagal syncope, I, like Dad, faint at hospitals at the sight of blood and upon hearing bad news, particularly on an empty stomach. By now I have learned to discern what is about to be a fleeting bout of light-headedness from a serious episode. I knew this was the big one. In the immortal words of TV's Fred Sanford, "Elizabeth, I'm coming!"

Regaining consciousness seconds later, I failed to comprehend why the nurse was in a panic. What convulsions? Surely she was making too much of the situation to call it a seizure.

Later in the afternoon the neurology resident arrived with an entourage of interns and students. After a series of probing questions and tests of neurological soft signs for stroke, no amount of explanation convinced her that I had merely fainted. Yet I knew that fainting was my avocation, and I was well experienced. While seizures occur at random, fainting has a trigger; and in the present situation, I had several of them. Relentless, the neurology resident dismissed any insight I could provide and ordered a series of tests—carotid artery scan, EKG, blood sample, and echocardiogram. Rightfully concerned about accuracy and precision, she needed to be certain that a blood clot had not formed in my leg and made its way to my brain.

Georgetown Medical Center prides itself on the survival rate of transplant patients, so doctors leave nothing to chance and no stone unturned. I felt like I was in an episode of TV's *House*. Despite my objections, the resident proceeded to order an echocardiogram. My only experience with echocardiogram was the stress test performed on the treadmill during my presurgical examinations. One thing I knew for certain was that in my condition there was no way I would find myself walking a treadmill today or anytime in the immediate future.

Pastor Smith arrived simultaneously as the orderly wheeled the gurney around for my transport to X-ray. The pastor's arrival was fortuitous, bringing great comfort, as I had good reason to be concerned about both Carol and myself. We were able to have a brief prayer, and I felt comforted and secure. I preceded Pastor out of the room toward the gurney completely oblivious to that blasted backless hospital gown. OMG! I hope I didn't moon the pastor!

It had been an exhaustively eventful day, and by evening I was famished. I knew a proper diet was necessary for healing. So I insisted on solid food. The young food-service worker all but threw the tray in the door. That was my only encounter with less than compassionate care, save "Nurse Wretched," who confiscated my water because my lab numbers were slightly off. Nurse Wretched also restricted me to bed since she did not want any accidental falls on her watch. Indeed, she was the nurse who had HIPAA*ed* me. So I was very glad when her shift ended and she retreated to the recesses of her coven cave. I don't know what food was on the dinner plate, but from the smell, my stomach was having no part of it. I returned the metal plate cover and pushed it away.

In the late evening, as I lightly dozed, I heard my name whispered softly. The vision before me was angelic. It was beloved Elijah. He was a welcomed end to that terrible day. We spent the time heartily talking of breaking news and current events. Yet, I spoke not a whisper of the day's occurrences. I needed to draw my strength from Elijah. Certainly, if he came unglued, there was little hope for me keeping it together.

Thursday

I had been looking forward to this day since that momentous Sunday evening last spring. It was to be the day of my triumph. I should have been released to resume my life, but alas, it was not to be. Although I had been awakened and wheeled back to X-ray for a carotid artery scan at 2:30 a.m., I had yet to have the dreaded echocardiogram. Since I was to spend the day in captivity, I resolved to make the best of it. I like to pattern my life after Elijah. Driving in any foreign environment, Elijah has never been lost. Not because of his keen sense of direction but because of his approach to any difficult situation. He calmly makes it an adventure and an opportunity for a new experience.

The restriction on solid food had been lifted, however the watery gray eggs and undercooked Canadian bacon were totally unappetizing. I longed for my usual fresh fruit compote, decaf, and oatmeal pastry. The hospital's canned peaches were no substitute, and the coffee tasted like dishwater. I was concerned because I knew the importance of returning the digestive track to full function. Moreover, I needed the nutrients to ensure a speedy recovery. Charlotte was taking a half-day from work, so I entreated her to stop at my favorite buffet restaurant, Epicurean, for real fresh ground coffee, fruit, and Ensure. This substituted for the hospital lunch of a dry hamburger devoid of trimmings, which, like the previous breakfast and dinner, was totally unpalatable.

Charlotte taught me how to maneuver the hospital bed for leverage whenever I needed to stand. I felt strong and sensed no pain, so I made routine trips to the bathroom on my own to exchange the cranberry juice, Ensure, and ice water that had been my sustenance for the previous two days.

Before noon, the house neurologist and his entourage arrived with questions to ascertain the source of the so-called seizure. Satisfied with the answers, the posse exited, declaring it an isolated incident. The diagnosis was low blood pressure syncope, which is sophisticated medical terminology for fainting. I still remember the neurology resident's disdainful glare as she had to acknowledge that I had been right all along.

As they departed, I overheard the neurologist exclaim that it was so hot in that room, he, too, would have fainted. I thought perhaps this meant I could go home today. But the attending physician was insistent on that darn echocardiogram. I was pleased that the nice young technician brought the machinery to my bed and I didn't have a stress test on the treadmill. As I well expected, there were no abnormalities to be found.

When the nurse arrived to exchange the intravenous tube that was threaded into a vein in my right wrist, we thought that the solution was not feeding into the vein but into the tissue beneath the skin. Removing the needle caused a great gush of blood that soaked my gown as well as the sheets that, after three days, needed to be freshened anyway.

In light of the superior skill and acumen of the surgical, nursing, and technical staff, I was struck by the unsanitary practices of some support staff. A glove dispenser and hand sanitizer hung on the inside wall of the doorway. As she entered, every nurse was careful to slip on a fresh pair of gloves and use the hand sanitizer. But the technician, who was of foreign extraction, never followed the procedure. He traveled from patient to patient and room to room, pushing his cart and taking vital signs while donning the same pair of purple latex gloves. I intended to speak up, but each time, once I remembered, he was long gone. Similarly, the housekeeping crew arrived on schedule but, without sweeping or vacuuming, sloshed the floor with a heavy rope mop dipped in the same dirty solution used in the previous rooms. The piece of trash dropped by the technician on Day 1 was pushed from one side of the room to the other.

Marvin visited and brought along Carol's friend Lisa. Lisa is a minister who was a kidney donor for her brother ten years earlier. She and I made a wonderful spiritual connection, sharing the events of our lives that led to the study of religion and to the donation. Pastor Davis, from Cony's church, also paid a visit. Each successive visitor brought gaiety and pleasure. Friends and family who could not visit kept the phone line busy. Others, who were reluctant to disturb my rest and recovery, sent love and well wishes through their prayers.

Undergoing a surgical procedure depletes your energy. So I spent the entire day in bed except for a lap around the surgical ward with Charlotte's assistance. This gave the staff the opportunity to change the linens. I returned to be pleasantly surprised by the arrival of Pastor Smith for a second visit. As much as I was pleased to see him, returning to my room, I was disturbed to observe the housekeeper exiting while reaching toward my iPhone that was curiously placed at the foot of the newly made bed. Mouth agape, when she glimpsed my presence, she retreated and scurried away. Patients should not leave their possessions unguarded. Opportunists come in the form of hospital staff, not to mention visitors.

By 5:30 p.m., it was apparent I was not going to be released today. The doctor was awaiting results of the echocardiogram. Carol remained in the ICU, where she would be housed for the next two weeks. But today, I was told, she was resting comfortably, despite elevated blood pressure. Praises to God, it was not a heart attack after all.

During the afternoon, a medical student poked her head in and asked if I would consent to an interview for a class assignment about doctor-patient communication. I readily agreed, since by this time I had formed some definite opinions on the topic. She disappeared for a few minutes and to my astonishment, returned with the entire class, plus two instructors. They crammed into the sizzling room and posed their questions, but none about communication.

The students were more curious about the motivation to become a donor. In response to the inquiry about my reason, I seized the opportunity to publicly profess my motivations. I did not reveal the clandestine reason, which was the desire for a new adventure. Instead, I first expressed the noble reason, which was a desire to ensure a better quality of life for Carol. I disclosed the philosophical motivations, which included a wish to do something extraordinary, and the desire to share the gift of health, with which I had been abundantly blessed. I concluded with the hope that if I should be in need of an organ, someone would be a donor for me, and that my action would stimulate others to donate, particularly African Americans.

In light of Carol's condition and my fainting, I could not relinquish the opportunity to make suggestions regarding communication. Topping the list was the need of patients for a prompt response to their requests for information, HIPAA or not. HIPAA is not good for every patient, particularly organ donors. As an example, my state of mind, hence my recovery, hinged on the assurance that Carol was alive and alright. To a patient, withholding information suggests that something is wrong and causes excessive worry.

In addition, doctors should listen to patients. As a prime example, when I tried to explain my fainting to the neurology resident, my input was dismissed. I know that doctors walk a delicate tightrope with scientific knowledge on one side and intuition on the other. But they would do well to know that patients can provide insight that can bridge the gap. The challenge is knowing when to trust a patient's word. In my case, there had been no reason for doubt.

Finally, health professionals should talk to patients in the presence of a caretaker. Apart from the effects of their condition, patients are often consumed with worry, thus the ability to listen, comprehend, and remember are not optimal. More than one conversation may be necessary. If information is critical and essential, it should be written, particularly information about dosages and schedules. Most importantly, professionals should not dispense critical information immediately following surgery since it is apt to be forgotten due to brain fog from anesthesia.

The students were gratified for the suggestions, and I was grateful for the opportunity to teach. Given my background with disabilities and religious studies, the instructors thought it would be nice for me to teach their class on medical ethics. Actually, this is precisely what I aspire to do. As they exited, we all beamed with satisfaction.

Bored in my captive predicament, I attempted to give my brain some needed exercise. In my mind I composed a list of bedside items for every patient that I wished I had had the foresight to bring: cough drops, chewing gum, mints, hand sanitizer, lip balm, wet towels, Q-tips, magnifier (or reading glasses), sticky notes, pen/pencil, mirror, phone charger, iPod, eye mask, earplugs.

Later, as I lay resting and watching as visitors traipsed about the corridor, I sighted an elderly, neatly dressed woman. As our eyes met, we exchanged smiles, which she interpreted as an invitation for a visit. My night visitor was from Scotland. She had a pleasant accent to match her buoyant personality. To a complete stranger she told of her husband, who occupied the adjacent room and who was recovering from surgery for pancreatic cancer.

In divinity school, I tried to avoid the course in pastoral counseling. I rationalized that if I did not take the course, I could never find myself engaged in the practice. Perhaps I wear a countenance of compassion, because wherever I go, people seem to seek me out for advice. I'm seldom able to solve their problems, but I am a good listener and I can offer a spiritual perspective. Somehow they leave grateful, feeling optimistic and spiritually uplifted.

My visitor needed only an attentive and patient listener. Sensitive to her deep worry, I could offer no more than a sympathetic ear. Recalling how Dad had succumbed to liver and colon cancer, I was concerned for her husband. As she rattled on, knowing that death is sometimes in divine order, I prayed a silent prayer for her consolation. I believe she would have conversed for several hours had a nurse not interrupted on the false pretext of attending to my care.

Although I took no offense, the nurse apologized for the interruption. It was the nurse's intent to rescue me from an unwanted intruder. My visitor's intent was to provide a lonely patient with welcome company. From my perspective, I was grateful to be able to inspire hope in another human being. I wondered if it were divine order that I had not been released that day.

Friday

I awakened feeling even stronger than I had the day before, albeit not from having received a full ration of nourishment. I have never had a voracious appetite, but over the previous three days, there had scarcely been a meal where my intake was more than two bites of solid food. I feared I had developed an eating disorder.

This was not irrational fear. In his final days, Dad became anorexic. Following his surgery, he rationalized that his weight loss had caused his gums to shrink, and not being able to wear his dental plate, chewing was impossible. But even with pureed foods, soups, and broth, Dad could not digest his food. We surmised, and I believe it was confirmed, that scar tissue had formed as a result of surgery partially obstructing his intestinal tract.

Not only did I not have an appetite, my intestinal tract function showed no sign of being restored. But through my determination, nothing would prevent me from leaving the hospital today. Since patients are strongly encouraged to be as active as possible following surgery, I walked at least twenty robust laps around the corridor before noon. Dr. Verbesey stopped by to check the incisions and gave the thumbs-up. A representative of the Kidney Foundation arrived with greetings, a gift bag, and statements of gratitude. Ironically, it was I who owed gratitude since I had not incurred any debt for the entire procedure.

I loved the gift of a kidney-shaped pillow, which I nicknamed "Kay's Kidney." While I did not consider the donation a loss, the kidney pillow was a physical representation of what I had lovingly and willingly given. The gift bag also included a backpack, water bottle, pens, mints, silicone mood bracelets, and a journal, all emblazoned with the Kidney Foundation motto as a permanent memento.

The Kidney Foundation's motto is "Donate Life." It is a compelling catchphrase for families experiencing the sudden loss of a loved one. But it bears a different relevance to a living donor. I did not save Carol's life. Dialysis was a painful disruption, yet her life was sustained, albeit because of the transplant, it is probable that her life would be extended. Yet, I do not regard myself as any more heroic than the health professionals who performed the transplant. Perhaps we are all heroes, but equally so. Ironically, I am grateful for the opportunity to ease Carol's distress and deliver on a divine revelation. Rather than feeling exalted, actually, I feel humbled that God chose me for this purpose.

I endured an endless stream of visits from health professionals before being discharged. My transplant coordinator arrived with medications and instructions for home use. Oxycodone was to be taken as necessary along with a stool softener. I realized the reason for the delayed bowel restoration—beyond the fact that I hadn't eaten but a few teaspoons of solid food in the past three days. The side effects of oxycodone include constipation. The nurses had administered it around the clock so I would not feel pain from the surgery. I was hesitant to take the oxycodone. I worried that as a narcotic, it had the potential to cause addiction. However, I was wary that if I did not take it, pain might arise. I did not want to become dependent, so I resolved to manage any incipient pain without medication. Actually, the only pain was from coughing. Kay's Kidney was useful for pressing against the abdomen to control the sudden expansion of the severed muscles while coughing. She worked wonders.

Carol is a certified hypnotherapist. She had helped me prevent post-surgical pain twenty years earlier. She taught me how to auto-hypnotize by deep meditation, the power of positive thinking, and communing with Christ. This time, I sought a booster session, but Carol explained that I already possessed the power within. So, through faith, I surrendered the situation to God, and trusted that I was not called to this purpose to experience suffering.

Admittedly, after my release, I took a few pills as instructed, but not in response to significant pain. An unanticipated aftereffect is that, because I now have one kidney, I can no longer take particular pain medications called NSAIDs. NSAIDs are a class of Nonsteroidal Anti-Inflammatory Drugs, which include aspirin, ibuprofen, naproxen, and other prescribed or popular over-the-counter medications. NSAIDs are potentially harmful to the kidneys. So it is now my responsibility to monitor future prescriptions to avoid NSAIDs for life. I am able to take Tylenol, which is not an NSAID. But ironically, Tylenol is the single mediation that causes an allergic reaction. Fortunately, I rarely require so much as an aspirin in my daily undertakings.

In the early afternoon Charlotte arrived to drive me home. She assisted as I prepared for a shower. As I disrobed, she remarked that there were several bruises on my abdomen and back. Although I did not venture to examine the bruises, the shower was my first opportunity to observe the incisions. The incisions were longer than I expected. I rationalized that my bikini-wearing days were long gone anyway.

Although I could dress without assistance, I was afraid to bend over lest I dislodge some stitches. Charlotte assisted me with socks and shoes along with applause and saying "Yaaay" after each action, as if dressing a toddler. I indulged her humor because I knew she was trying to lift my spirit. Awaiting the release order, we cautiously strolled the hospital corridors to the ICU. Carol was alert, cheerful, and talkative. Charlotte snapped a photo of us together for Facebook.

From Carol's experience, I became aware that recovery for the transplant recipient is fraught with peril. The possibility of rejection of the new kidney is a serious concern. Carol was restrained to the ICU for two weeks until her vitals and lab results were stable. Although the kidney was healthy, it had not yet begun to function. Naturally, I was concerned. Distraught, I didn't know whether to feel anticipation or rejection.

Though cheerful, Carol's words suggested that she continued to mistrust her medical team. She was frustrated with the myriad tests and procedures and suggested that the doctors were ordering tests for the insurance payment. I countered that the doctors were behaving as they should, ensuring that she received thorough care. I proceeded to express that from this day forward, Carol now had a new lease on life that demanded a new attitude about health professionals. She needed to take seriously the treatments and medications with no more negative attitude. I was astonished that she accepted this admonishment from me, a younger sister. She overtly agreed, but I knew that long-held beliefs are difficult to extinguish.

The release order came around 5:30 p.m. But my elation was dampened by the uncertainty of leaving Carol in the ICU with her fate unclear. The amber sky blushed as I engulfed the fresh air. Daylight was fading as Charlotte and I drove past the monuments on the National Mall. The National Mall is an awe-inspiring place. One is humbled by the ambience, which exudes power, valor, and heroism. It is a permanent tribute to people who carved their place in history while contributing to the advancement of the nation. They were statesmen, soldiers, and martyrs, and all were men, save the iconic nurses at the Vietnam War Memorial. As we drove through the streets, I wondered why there were no tributes to people who had done extraordinary acts of humanitarianism. In answer, I concluded that those who were memorialized by monuments gained the praise of men. Humanitarians gain the favor of God.

As we caught sight of the helicopter landing on the White House lawn carrying the nation's first African American president, I thought of how I had never believed I would witness such a phenomenon in my lifetime. It was a hope of the future accomplished in the present. I recall standing for hours in the bitter cold to witness the inauguration and how I endured this on behalf of ancestors who had not lived to experience the occasion. I wondered what other new wonders there were to be accomplished. I hoped that, through my donation, I had ensured that Carol would be around to experience them.

I was starkly reminded that I had been oblivious to politics for the last several days. The drive symbolized a return to reality with a new beginning. But ironically, I was facing a new beginning with unhealed wounds from the recent past. I had come through favorably, but that was only half the battle. Carol's condition remained tenuous. These things weighed heavily on my mind until, returning to the house, I was uplifted by greetings from the gatehouse staff, who presented flowers and a fruit basket that had arrived during my absence.

Ahh! It was great to be in *my* bed, the place where this journey had begun six months ago. If my home is my castle, then my bed is my throne. Fatigued, I only wanted to curl up and sleep. Charlotte prepared a light dinner of soup and salad. Though still without an appetite, I managed to eat a few bites and wash them down with Ensure.

Following dinner, Charlotte settled in the guest room to watch the opening ceremony of the Winter Olympics in Sochi, Russia. I could hear her talking to the television. Charlotte makes a social event of her television viewing, laughing aloud and talking to the characters. But entertainment held no interest for me. For me, "That's all she wrote." Like a newborn kitten, I slept through the night for the first time in three days.

Saturday

Saturday morning I awoke to the refreshing aroma of my favorite Café du Monde decaf. Still lacking an appetite, I was grateful for the fresh fruit Charlotte had prepared. I must have slept most of the morning because I cannot recall anything of significance except that Elijah arrived bearing the special edition leather-bound Jeremiah Study Bible, insisting that I needed to have it immediately.

Later in the afternoon, as I lay watching the Olympic women's skiathlon, Midge phoned to relate that she and Millie were on the outskirts of town. I was not really in a mood to entertain houseguests, but there was no dissuading big sisters who had driven all night determined to witness for themselves that Carol and I were alright and to assist with whatever we needed.

Perhaps it stems from vanity and pride, but I don't enjoy people making a fuss over me. People describe me as independent, headstrong, and immensely private. This is particularly true when I'm feeling ill, and today was no exception. My sisters' arrival presented the opportunity for me to leave bed and sit in the living room for a lively chat.

Crabs are a family delight, so Millie and Midge prepared a dinner of Maryland blue crabs, steamed shrimp, and corn on the cob. Of course, no one can eat crabs without drinking beer. Since beer taken in moderation does not harm the kidney, I lightly indulged. But not even crabs and beer could stimulate an appetite, so after a few bites, light-headed, I excused myself from the table. I have no recollection of when Millie and Midge retired that night. They would remain in town a few days and return to Atlanta on Tuesday immediately ahead of another nasty winter storm.

Sunday

Sunday morning I awakened early feeling clammy and cold. Millie and Midge prefer to sleep in the cold. I, on the other hand, prefer warm and cozy. So far, Millie and Midge had not had much of an opportunity to assist in caretaking. Millie is a gourmet cook, but, of course, I wanted none of her usual lavish meals. Midge and I enjoyed the Sunday church service through live-streaming.

In the prayer requests, Pastor announced that I was home resting peacefully. Few people knew about the surgery, and most who did thought it was a minor procedure.

Charlotte arrived in the afternoon to escort Millie and Midge to the hospital to visit Carol. I felt guilty about not going, but I had no desire to see the inside of a hospital again for a very long time. I seized this opportunity to enjoy a refreshing shower. I was careful not to disturb the incisions. Emerging from the shower, towel in hand, I had the first occasion to observe my full body in the mirror. Besides the incisions, there were bruises and a map sketched in black ink on my skin. It appeared as if I had been the victim of an alien abduction and probe. The sight was so overwhelming that I again felt light-headed. So I eased myself to the plushness of the bathroom carpet. Through the door I heard my sisters preparing to exit, and from that position on the floor, I eked out a feeble goodbye.

I soon regained composure and stumbled back to bed. Cony and wife Liz arrived after church bearing a complete home-cooked Sunday dinner and yet another fruit basket. Too weary to sit and chat, I retired to the bedroom for the remainder of the evening. The family made a circle around my bed to say grace and left me with a full-course Southern-style dinner of baked Cornish hen, wild rice and gravy, fresh vegetables, a crispy salad, and apple pie. I devoured my first balanced meal in many days.

Aftermath

In the first week following surgery, time was spent engaging in the same routine daily—resting, sleeping, and scarcely eating though loyal to the ritual of drinking Ensure and two liters of water a day. I arose at my regular time and made the bed so I would not be tempted to return to it. I showered, groomed, and dressed in street clothes and made the daily trek to the mailbox. I had invested in several flowing caftan dresses, soft cotton T-shirts, and elastic-waist velour pants in various vibrant colors. Since I detested daytime television, I viewed a few unremarkable movies plus a full season of *Star Trek: Deep Space Nine*, a gift from a colleague. I read occasionally, especially the

Jeremiah Study Bible, which I loved. Frequent visits to the bathroom were painful despite laxatives and other preparations to restore bowel function.

Tuesday marked the one-week anniversary of surgery and my follow-up appointment. Abandoning chic, I dressed in the first thing that fell out of the closet. To avoid disrupting the workday of those who would have willingly provided transportation, I called for a driver to take me to the Transplant Center. As a courtesy for donors, I always had a very brief wait. The nurse took the usual vital signs and ushered me to the examination room. I was feeling fine and the incisions were healing well, so the appointment took all of 15 minutes.

Dr. Verbesey inquired about Carol's status. It occurred to me that since we had separate surgical teams and because of HIPAA, not even the doctors knew the disposition of the other's case. Following the appointment, I paid a visit to Carol in the ICU, then helped myself to the buffet at Epicurean. Carol was in good spirits and doing well although the kidney had yet to commence functioning. We talked of various matters, especially her progress. In some ways, her recovery was more rapid than my own.

After one week and a day, on Wednesday my bowel finally kicked in. Praise God! By Thursday, I felt like phoning friends I had meant to contact before surgery. Out of sheer boredom, at some point, I opened the laptop and checked my email. There were few messages of substance, so I responded only to the ones that required immediate attention. I received occasional calls and cards from church members, plus several lovely bouquets. My dean was especially kind in making a donation in my honor to the Black Science Fiction Foundation since she knew I was a Star Trek Trekkie.

By Friday, with a rolling basket, I was ready to take the one-block excursion on foot to the grocery store. The slushy snow from the recent storm was no obstacle. Once inside, I was overcome by the insufferably high temperature in the deli area, which I had never sensed before. Waiting to be served, once again, I felt light-headed. I hoped this was not to become a frequent occurrence and that it was not an omen for a new physical anomaly brought on by the absence of a kidney. By this time, I was taking medication occasionally, mostly in anticipation of pain upon physical activity such as walking to the store.

During the weeks of recovery, cooking was out of the question, and despite the few meals I had enjoyed, I could feel myself losing weight, albeit in the wrong places. Neighbors visited and offered to go shopping, but there was nothing I needed or wanted. Elijah was kind to bring dinner on several occasions, even through the snow and ice. Yogurt was a staple of every meal. Women know this is important after taking antibiotics.

Although I still ate like a bird, I longed for an evening out at a nice restaurant. Interestingly, each of the girlfriends reneged on their promise to take me to dinner, offering one excuse after another. At times like these, you can really find out about friends. Some people feel they need to give you space. Others simply cannot make room in their lives. I wondered if there were times I had neglected or slighted friends—probably very many, so I did not hold a grudge. I am fortunate to have Elijah and a loving family.

In exactly two weeks, I turned a corner physically. The weather since the surgery had been particularly nasty. It snowed every few days. When I could no longer bear the cabin fever, I set out for the gym. Fortunately, I had to go no further than to the elevator and across the lobby. The first day, I clocked one-half mile on the treadmill then strolled along the waterfront promenade watching the waves and meditating. Returning to the gym daily, I regained more energy from each visit.

I needed to get back in shape because I was working toward the cruise I had planned, which was so important to my psychological recovery. Until I knew I was physically strong, I delayed booking until the last minute. By now walking the treadmill up to a mile a day, I felt fully prepared. Previously, in October, Mary displayed an interest in going along on the cruise. But now, whenever I brought up the question, she changed the topic. I knew I couldn't take the cruise alone, so I asked Myke. Even though she is retired, she was hesitant to commit for the full seven days.

Major obstacles to post-surgical recovery are depression and fatigue. In hindsight, I would add hypochondria to the list. Fatigue wants to rule the day. But it is imperative not to submit. I overcame fatigue by setting goals, plus having determination. Having goals and a reward to work toward were the best motivators. My goal was to leave the hospital on Thursday. Since that was not possible, I was determined to leave Friday. So I worked at it by walking laps around the surgical wing. Now the cruise was my crowning reward.

Mind over matter, spirit over flesh; although it seems counterintuitive, movement and physical activity are extremely important to combat fatigue. A donor has the advantage of excellent health before surgery. Therefore, the presurgery health status can be quickly recovered. A major key to recovery is not to accept an attitude of illness and fall into a pattern of lethargy. The urge to remain immobile must be overcome by the sheer force of determination. I made it a challenge by taking charge and quickly returning to daily routines.

Drinking lots of water is a requisite. Since residual anesthesia is the main culprit in fatigue, water is necessary to flush it from the body. I have heard that it may take up to six months to completely remove all traces of anesthesia from the brain cells.

The support of caregivers and others is also essential. Elijah insisted on sponsoring the cruise as his show of support and admiration, and his emotional support meant the world to me. While independence is a virtue and a catalyst for recovery, I knew that assistance from others must be cheerfully accepted. However, this is difficult for me. So, even when I believed I could do it myself, I accepted the generous offers of assistance from others.

Having to accept assistance is an unknown sensation to me, but I'm working on improving. For example, I haven't always been a seasoned traveler. In high school, I competed for the student exchange program, Experiment in International Living. I weathered each round and became a finalist for study abroad in Holland. The cost of $1,100 was almost three months' worth of Dad's salary. So I dared not ask for it and forfeited the opportunity, fully knowing that one day money would no longer be an obstacle to the achievement of my dreams.

That day arrived when I was a graduate student. I secured a grant to conduct research in four nations in the Caribbean. I had not traveled alone since the first flight to Syracuse the day I had left home for college. I was apprehensive in anticipation of lonely meals in hotel restaurants, and depending on the goodness of strangers.

In a corner of the restaurant of a small villa in St. Croix, two older gentlemen at the neighboring table struck up a conversation with a young, attractive female too naive to be fearful. As it turned out, they were officers on a Trinidadian oil tanker. As we talked into the evening, they were pleasantly impressed as I held my own in debate over world politics.

That conversation proved to be most memorable. I enjoyed gaining their respect for my intellect. As I retreated to my room, there was no request for my phone number or salacious invitation for further contact. Instead what greeted me was the fact that my room had been looted by the crew of sailors next door who had crossed the adjoining balcony to gain entry. My research equipment with all the data were taken. When the officers learned this, all my belongings were returned together with a heartfelt apology.

From this incident, I learned how to graciously accept the assistance of others, accept that sometimes we must rely on people who are stronger and more powerful and have the means to obtain results we cannot achieve for ourselves. Refusing a sincere offer from someone blocks their blessing by denying them the opportunity of reaping the benefit of generosity. Moreover, when we are assured that there are others to assist us, we are less fearful to endeavor new ventures.

On that trip, I also found that I liked myself, and realized that I'm actually very good company. I now actually don't mind traveling alone because it forces me to depend on others and seek new sources of interesting conversation. Even when I don't speak the language, I love creating ways to communicate. Although these personal traits appear somewhat harsh, they are precisely what made me a successful donor and propelled me to a speedy recovery. With self-determination and gracious assistance, I was back to health within and ready to sail in three weeks.

Giving, Forgiving, and Thanksgiving

Ever since I was old enough to spell the word, I had wanted to be a philanthropist. But being from a hardworking African American family, I was more likely to be on the receiving side of the generosity continuum.

I will always step forward to support the American Red Cross. As I left junior high school that bitter cold day in January, I was met by Dad on his way to the school speaking words strange to my ears. Like the crowd's reaction to the disciples on the Day of Pentecost, when Dad informed me that my house burned down, I thought he had been drinking. But it was too early in the day for that, and I witnessed firsthand the charred remains of what had previously been our warm, love-filled townhouse on Atlantic Avenue in Brooklyn, New York.

A four-year-old boy playing with matches in his home six doors away had accidentally lit the curtains. The water in the fire hydrants froze, and the firefighters could do little to contain the flames that demolished an entire block of homes. That afternoon the family gathered one by one at the precinct station to await our fate. The young ones were given toys left over from the Christmas toy drive. This was well before the advent of cellphones, so it was impossible to reach Midge at her job in Manhattan. Arriving home in late evening, at the sight of the catastrophe, she dropped all her bags and screeched in horror.

The headline for the evening news was that the Long Island Railroad, the lifeline for suburban white businessmen who worked in the city, was delayed because of the thick black smoke. There was no display of sympathy for the working-class black families who had lost the few possessions they owned. As our family was split apart and scattered in various directions to live with relatives, it was the compassion of the American Red Cross that provided the foundation for us to put our lives back together.

Growing up, we lacked money to engage in music, dance, art, or sports activities. So it was incumbent on us to use what had been bestowed by God—our intellect. As a result, I attended an elite college not by affirmative action but by meritorious academic achievement. Yet, undoubtedly, it required the generosity of academic scholarships. But as my siblings and I excelled in academics, many creative talents and potential were forfeited.

Throughout life, I've had outstanding role models for generosity. Many years ago, I had lunch with Dave Winfield, the famed Major League Baseball outfielder. Now retired, Dave is a great humanitarian. Throughout my years,

I had encountered scores of millionaires but none with such generosity and sincere passion for the improvement of the human condition as Dave. His desire to give and his love of humanity were genuine, not for show or for self-aggrandizement. As he spoke of his benevolent endeavors, the tenor of his spirit resonated with my soul. I doubted if I would ever possess anything that could be given with such a pure and loving heart. Yet I ached for the opportunity. I imagined winning the lottery and knew exactly what to do with the bounty. I dreamed of creating a foundation in honor of my parents to make grants to underprivileged children to develop their creative talents.

In later years later as a professional, I achieved my dream of becoming that philanthropist, but not in the way I imagined. Early in my career, I discovered that I possess a talent for grant-writing. Today, having garnered more than $10 million, I have singularly generated fellowships for more than 100 students for graduate education. Through these grants, I became an accidental philanthropist. I realized that my charitable foundation was me—through the use of my creative gifts.

Generosity is not without drawbacks. There are specific character traits that must exist alongside this virtue. Forgiveness is a close cousin that must travel in tandem with generosity. For indeed, with generosity, there is the strong potential for being misunderstood and misused. And this will require the exercise of forgiveness. Generally, I am forgiving, but it just takes longer for some things.

After the first twelve years of successful grant writing, I desired a career change to a more stable occupation, so I secured a lucrative position at a professional organization. I knew within the first month that I would was not cut out for that environment. I had no intention of becoming a party to the competitive, cut-throat, impersonal culture. True to my prediction, within one year, I was totally blindsided with the proclamation that my position had been eliminated.

My firing from that job was not precipitous. As supervisor, I had encountered overt opposition from a subordinate associate who hurled a racial slur. Ironically, this trouble led to *my* dismissal. The firing was devastating, and naturally my mind entertained the urge to retaliate.

Fortunately, I immediately secured a more rewarding position as a professor that allowed me to utilize my creative talents in a more relaxed atmosphere. Ironically, the same associate who instigated the firing became my student. I could have exacted revenge and the student knew it. Although the student did not confess or ask for it, I chose to exercise forgiveness. I sensed that the individual was penitent and never intended to cause me to lose my job. Besides, forgiveness was made easier because the devastation of being fired was cushioned by a generous separation settlement, together with the knowledge that I was liberated from an environment I had no business working in the first place. In light of it all, I like to say that's the best place I ever got fired from.

Upon graduation, my former associate secured a position with a granting agency, and through the desire to make restitution, facilitated my receipt of several substantial grants. Because I chose forgiveness, my generosity and philanthropic efforts were advanced, and this became a reason for praise and thanksgiving.

Forgiving is a complicated process. It is commonly believed that a person cannot truly forgive unless the insult is completely forgotten. Well, I can attest that I am not in command of what I forget. If that were the case, I would not be presently lamenting the onset of the aging process. I maintain that, instead, forgiveness is an attitude adjustment relating to the motives underlying our actions and interactions toward someone who has dealt an insult. For example, to exact punishment or revenge is an act of *un*-forgiveness.

However, dissociation can be an acceptable forgiveness response toward one who has caused serious injury. Victims of domestic violence, abuse, neglect, sexual molestation, and assault are within the realm of righteousness to remove that source of insult from their lives and not restore an injurious relationship. So rather than contempt, forgiveness would entail changing the heart of the offended, leaving retribution for the offender to divine justice. Certainly, it may not come easily or immediately, but with the proper relationship with God, the hurt can be healed. To cite a famous quote from Martin Luther King Jr.: "The arc of the moral universe is long, but it bends toward justice."

There have been other times when my generosity required forgiveness. It is particularly challenging to forgive when an insult is dealt from within the church. I loved church and had been active in the various ministries and activities. With the compensation from the dismissal, I desired to tithe the financial windfall. As a research investigator, I decided to establish a scholarship for deserving graduate students conducting theses and dissertations. I am a strong supporter of African American investigators who bring cultural perspective and balance to the research world. I deplore the plethora of flawed research that perpetuates myths of inequality and upholds subjugation of African American people. I believe that the realities of Black existence can only be accurately presented by African Americans themselves. The graduate research scholarship perfectly reflected my passion.

The terms of the scholarship were established. Announcement of the availability of scholarships was to be made through the church newsletter for a brief period. I was away on travel for most of the announcement period. I returned to notice that other scholarships had been announced with the exception of mine, and consequently, there were no applicants. The bizarre conversation with the committee representative led me to conclude that my scholarship was not announced as a way to prevent me from grandstanding my financial success. (What did they know of the awful circumstance under which it had been acquired?) Of course, grandstanding was the furthest thought from my mind. Disgusted and crestfallen, I stormed out of the church doors, vowing never to return.

I wandered, devastated and spiritually lost for several years. Searching for spiritual nourishment, I found my way to divinity school. I have since forgiven and returned to church, albeit dissociated from the offending individual. I don't think about the situation until the scholarships are awarded each year. This act of forgiveness was critical, for had the situation not occurred, the relationship I share with God today, which I sought as a result of being out of fellowship that led me to divinity school, and which eventually precipitated the kidney donation, would not have fruition.

The troubles of our lives serve to promote spiritual advancement as well as build character for fulfilling our divine purpose. When we meet frustrations and disappointments, it might mean that we are following our own mind rather than God's command. But God has a way of turning even our worse mess into a positive outcome.

So during my times of strife, I continued to tithe and resisted the temptation to withdraw from God or abandon faith. Tithing is an act of generosity. Many people reason that they cannot tithe until their finances are in order. I maintain that one's finances will never be in order *until* they tithe. As a result, I can attest that the troubles of my life served to draw me closer to God. And through my ordeals, I experienced spiritual growth and became the instrument of God's grace for Carol's life.

The following excerpt from a poem written by Mother Teresa captures the essence for giving, forgiving, and thanksgiving:

People are often unreasonable, irrational, and self-centered
Forgive them anyway

If you are kind, people may accuse you of selfish, ulterior motives
Be kind anyway

You see, in the final analysis, it is between you and God;
It is not about you and them anyway.

For an organ donor, the ultimate reward is the sense of accomplishment and the joy that comes from fulfilling God's purpose.

Brazil

Brussels, Belgium

Great Wall China

Egypt

Family Reunion

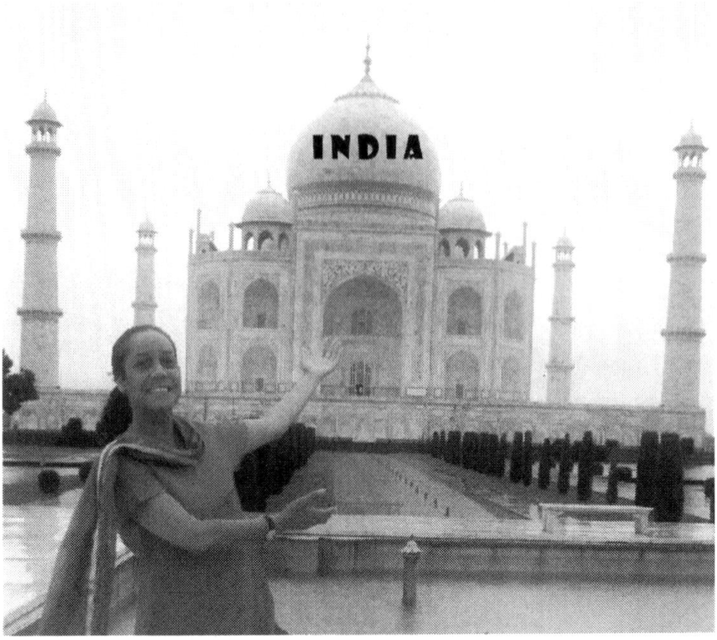
INDIA

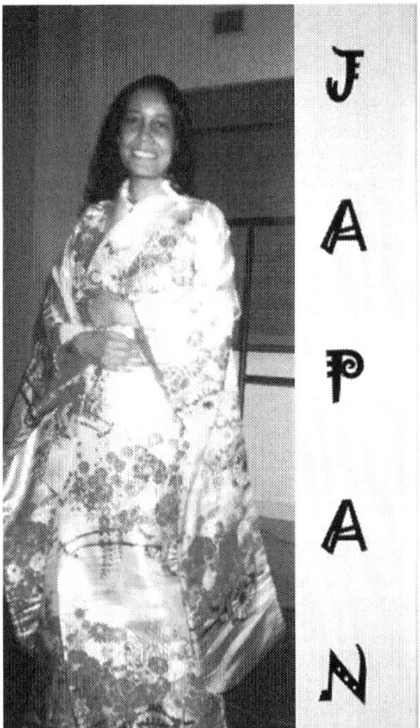
JAPAN

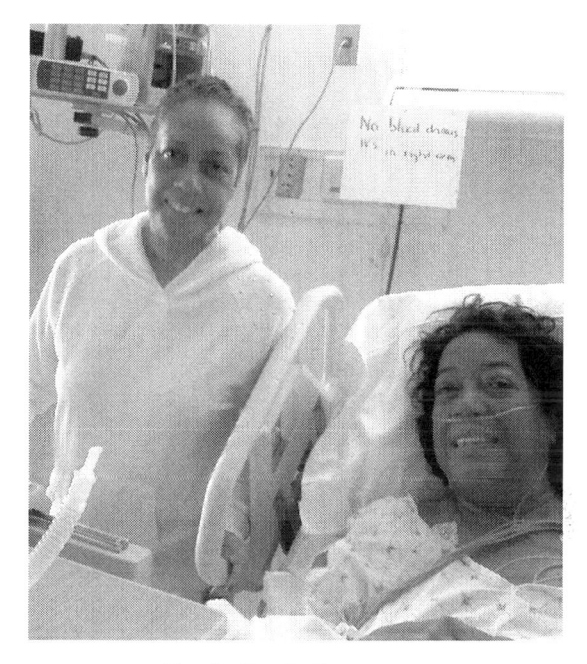

Kay & Carol after surgery

Kenya

56

Sisters
Clockwise: Faye, Myke Carol, Millie, Marcella, Kay, Charlotte, Midge

Strength to Strength

The Old Testament concept of *anastasis* refers to an awakening, especially a miraculous recovery from illness. Carol's recovery was more tenuous than mine. At times, I wondered if the kidney would ever start to function.

Carol and I realized that for the kidney to accept its new life and function, there needed to be a new consciousness—total release from me, and acceptance and appreciation from Carol. We could not view it as merely an organ, a piece of flesh or physical thing but a miraculous Godsend, a fulfillment of purpose, a culmination of all the events of our lives and the beginning of spiritual uplifting. During one moment in daily meditation, I sent a prayer to the kidney. I released it and willed it to accept its new home as if it were still inside my body. To reflect our sentiment Carol and I assigned her the name Anastasia, which translated means *Resurrection*.

Three weeks post-surgery, I was well into recovery, but inside Carol, Anastasia had yet to live up to her name. Yet, we did not relinquish hope or trust. Valentine's Day arrived and, among other gifts I received, a floral bouquet from Carol was a lovely gesture. Thoughtfully, since she was still confined to the ICU, she had preordered it before the surgery. Finally, after the third week, Carol was transferred from the ICU to the post-surgery wing. I visited her again, bringing bedside toiletries and other necessities. When I arrived, one of her mystical friends was performing a healing ritual and providing a foot bath. Carol had begun to develop blisters on her heels from lying in bed. In all the weeks of her hospitalization, Carol had not received a proper bath, and blisters appeared on her heels.

During my visit, a most unusual East Indian doctor arrived. Instead of the typical white lab coat or scrubs, he wore a gray suit, and from his manner and conversation, I wondered if he was a doctor at all or some well-meaning impostor. This doctor had an extremely personal bedside manner. Carol mentioned that he recommended that she become a mentor to a needy youth, advice that I found to be curious medicine for a transplant recipient. But his methods and practices were in concert with Carol's belief in nontraditional treatment, and Carol adored him.

He remained with Carol longer, and was more personally involved in her situation than any other doctors. Although he was not a psychiatrist, his treatment was mostly concerned with her emotional state. The only medical procedure I saw him perform was a cursory examination of her throat with only a penlight. Upon our introduction, he shook my hand and complimented me on my generosity and unselfishness. Because he was so unusually kind and benevolent, I wondered if he might not be an angel in the flesh. Carol would later confirm that he was truly a physician, but I still had my doubts.

After three weeks of hospitalization, Carol was experiencing eating problems. In the ICU she found the hospital food inedible. Carol has always been extremely cautious of the foods she eats and avoids, preferring fresh organic fruits and vegetables. So she asked me to contact her patient advocate to arrange for meals that were more in concert with her preference. Later, during the third week, when I visited her on the surgery floor, she was eating regularly and even looking forward to meals.

That was my final visit to Carol in the hospital. Although Anastasia had yet to take hold, Carol was finally out of the ICU and stable. I embarked upon the Imagination in the Port of Baltimore on Sunday, after nineteen days of recovery. Mary had worked out her indecision and we cruised along the eastern coastline to the warm sunny waters of the Caribbean. I was feeling strong and well on the way to complete recovery. The cruise was precisely what I needed, that is, healing, relaxation, and no worry from the outside world. We spent seven days enjoying peace and rest.

After four weeks and a snow day, I returned to the office. It felt as though I had never been away. Few colleagues knew about the surgery, and those who knew respected my privacy and didn't pester me for details. The daily health walk between home, office, and the Metro in the crisp winter air was revitalizing. I did not experience the fatigue that often accompanies recovery. However, since the brain is the final frontier for recovery, I found I had forgotten small details such as where files were located as well as how to conduct some automatic routines that I had performed many times.

I returned to fitness training, and one morning after a fierce workout, in anticipation of pain, I ventured to take oxycodone. It was then I discovered the cause of my light-headedness. Hours later in the office, feeling dizzy and nauseous, I helped myself to the carpeted floor. Returning home, I did what I should have done many weeks earlier, which was to dump those pills down the drain.

Months before surgery, I had consented to travel to California to conduct a workshop. Now, I regretted that decision because it meant packing, lifting luggage, and trudging long concourses to make airport connections, not to mention standing to deliver a three-hour lecture one day and a five-hour lecture the next.

Visiting with Gloria, my great friend and mentor, was a benefit of the trip. Gloria is my idol. She fearlessly travels to every corner the globe. In more youthful days, Gloria invited me to Saudi Arabia to teach in a graduate program she established through her university in California. As African American women in an Islamic, theocratic environment, we enjoyed testing the limits of the boundaries imposed upon women. Gloria had lived in Saudi Arabia for years at a time and was thoroughly familiar with the culture and connected to the right powerful people. Together, with Gloria in the lead, we roamed unescorted and undaunted through the city devoid of the traditional black head scarf, entering restaurants reserved for men and sampling the fruity tobacco "shisha" pipe just for the experience. We even found a way to enjoy wine, a favorite past-time of both of us.

Soon after my arrival in California, Charlotte texted to report that Carol was released from the hospital. After four weeks, Anastasia had finally begun to function. Like her original owner, she had a mind of her own and needed to be cherished as a gift of God with full acknowledgement of the spiritual force that facilitated her transfer to Carol.

In California, Gloria and I enjoyed a lovely dinner on a mountaintop overlooking San Jose until the city lights dotted the landscape. The trip was great for my recovery and visiting friends was better than having them visit me. This signaled that both Carol and I had recovered. We could finally exhale. My adventure had come to a close with no residual physical or psychological side effects.

Despite all, Carol had not really eaten well in the hospital. She lost weight and seemed feeble and tired. She had been confined to bed for more than a month and needed physical therapy to restore her muscle function. Her doctors arranged a week in a rehabilitation facility near home before she could return to daily life.

Carol enjoyed the time in the rehabilitation facility. She had mandatory physical therapy, and good nutritious meals were eaten in the dining room, where she relished the social interactions. She met interesting people and formed a bond with her roommate, who was a retired nurse. She practiced life skills to help manage life upon her return home.

Cony built an additional handrail on the stairway of her home so she could have additional support when she climbed the stairs. Meanwhile, Marcella thoroughly scoured the house and repainted so the environment would be bacteria free for Carol's diminished immune system.

After a brief time at home, Carol was readmitted to the hospital. At one of her required weekly follow-up visits, her creatinine count was elevated. It was discovered that Anastasia had signs of BK virus. This type of infection, whose moniker is the initials for an unpronounceable foreign name, is not uncommon after a kidney transplant and taking immunosuppressant drugs. Apparently there was an error in the prescription for one of the medications, which resulted in Carol receiving less than the appropriate dosage.

For Carol and me, each new crisis was another scare that the outcome might not be successful. But through it all, I held faith that God's command was not designed to result in disappointment or failure.

After a long and harsh winter, spring was slow to advance. Too many hours had been spent perched in the secure comfort of my sofa watching the courtyard turn into a winter wonderland. In mid-April, the cherry blossoms had yet to grace the Washington tidal basin and the leaves had barely begun to bud. The pear tree outside my balcony, from which Cony and Charlotte had harvested dozens of pears the previous October, sprouted few white blossoms. The squirrels, not finding any other tasty treats, feasted on the meager blossoms that did appear.

Weeks later, at long last, spring arrived, marking a complete cycle since my divine revelation. In May, Carol reached 100 days post-surgery with no further complications. May is the month of Carol's birthday, so we had many blessings for which to give praise at the family prayer gathering. I realized that it was resilience that got me through those 100 days. During the moments of despair, I used sheer determination to cast off the negatives and return to equilibrium.

To be sure, Carol is not out of the woods yet, and she may never truly reach that status. She must take the immunosuppressant drugs for the rest of her life and endure any side effects. Even then, there is always a possibility of rejection, which would require a return to dialysis or another transplant. Because of her weakened immune system, she is susceptible to a multiplicity of opportunistic diseases.

Despite all that, the quality of Carol's life is much improved by the sheer matter of not having to spend half her life in dialysis. What is most observable is the improvement in her energy level and cognitive function. Carol has always been exuberant and creative. Anastasia and the accompanying sense of gratitude, plus the expectation of a healthy life lifted Carol's spirit tremendously. As for me, through a biological process known as compensatory renal hypertrophy, my remaining kidney will enlarge and increase in function, leaving no residual consequence in the absence of Anastasia. I require no medications, and there are no aftereffects of the surgery, save three slowly fading scars and occasional itchiness.

In our conversations, Carol and I often pause to reflect on what we have gained. We came to realize that although dialysis is a miraculous, lifesaving procedure, it is nonetheless imperfect and can never replace the living organ that God created. Yet without Carol's need for dialysis, and my mandate to be a donor, we would have not paused to appreciate God's purpose in the creation of *two* kidneys. Through the vehicle of our family prayer sessions, we continually communicate this appreciation to God.

Prayer

Twenty years before the transplant, following Mom and Dad's departure, the siblings felt it necessary to devise a means to maintain family cohesion. We are a large family of eleven surviving siblings and four generations comprised of a score of nieces and nephews dispersed throughout five states. Thus, it is easy to splinter and proceed in many separate directions. The idea for a regular prayer gathering came to Carol shortly after Mom's departure. It was born of the recognition that we each had individual needs that required divine intervention and family support.

When the prayer gatherings began, we were not certain that they would be sustained. In the beginning we were not cognizant of each other's prayer practices or depth of spirituality. So we decided to give prayer a chance by meeting together in local clusters one Sunday each month, rotating at various residences for a home-cooked meal. Carol adapted the "Mastermind Prayer Method," a communal, intercessory prayer ritual created by Jack Boland. A printed list reflecting each family member's prayer request is dispersed prior to the session. Even though we gather in clusters in different locations, we share the same list and focus on the same earthly and heavenly manifestations.

As our family prayer gatherings show, there is still truth to the hackneyed adage "The family that prays together stays together." Prayer Sunday is more than a family social gathering. During the early years, we prayed for personal needs. We witnessed one by one as our prayers were miraculously answered. Some might think this was luck, but I was thoroughly convinced of the power of prayer through the experience of my older brother Kelvin.

Born with cerebral palsy, Kelvin, affectionately known as "Bro" for "Little Brother," was dependent on the nurture of Mom for his existence. After Mom's departure, his boarding house arrangement failed to work out, and unknown to the family, he found himself in a homeless shelter. In prayer sessions, as Bro prayed for a place of his own, I thought his prayer would be in vain, as surely this was obviously not God's purpose for his life.

Pie in my face! How arrogant to think I could know God! Because of his disability, Bro was rescued from the homeless shelter and relocated in a group home by the kind and compassionate missionaries of the Lt. Joseph P. Kennedy Institute. Today he resides independently and with utter dignity in a neatly kept condo in Maryland. He makes his way to church on public transportation through any weather condition and has never missed a family prayer session.

Carol had the original idea for the prayer sessions, but indeed it was Bro who insisted we carry out the plan. If not for his insistence, we would not have begun, nor would we have sustained these sessions that have been the mainstay of family unity. In two decades, we have scarcely missed a session.

Over the years, we have discovered that the purpose and key to an effective prayer life is to align our will with God's purpose for our lives. Our focal scripture from the Gospel of Mathew reminds us that when we are in accord with God, whatever is bound on earth will be bound in heaven, and whatever is loosed on earth will also be loosed in heaven, and whenever two or three are gathered in his name, Christ is there in the midst.

On that momentous Sunday, seven months before the surgery, the family prayed for miraculous healing of Carol's kidney condition. Also, in my personal daily meditations, it had been my prayer to be used in the perfecting of God's will. While I beseeched God for intervention for Carol, I knew that for my prayer to be sincere, I would have to be willing to be part of the plan. My prayer resulted in this divine revelation and the spiritual uplift of the family.

Family
Sisters are not the same as friends. My sisters stand by me right or wrong to a fault. I know I can never get an objective opinion from a sister, because she will always

be on my side. Sisters vicariously feel your happiness, sorrow, grief, and much more. Sisters are encouragers. We remind one another how awesome we are.

With sisters there can be no pretentions. They know you better than you know yourself. At times, they can cause embarrassment by revealing the dumb things you did that you'd never disclose even to the closest friend. For example, every Thanksgiving we draw gales of laughter by evoking the memory of the time Carol was dispersed to the market to purchase the snack crackers needed for our favorite hors d'oeuvre dip. Expecting bruschetta, or at least Wheat Thins, we roared as Carol served the dip with Zwiebacks! (Zwiebacks are baby teething crackers).

People say we look alike. But we know that each one is an individual. We are a rainbow of sizes, body builds, complexions, personalities, and hair lengths and textures. Mom was a "Georgia Redbone," a mixture of Native American, African, and European ancestry. Dad had a similar mixed heritage but with a greater prominence of African American features. They met as young adults in North Carolina where she worked in the tobacco industry and he was a singer in a traveling quartet.

Not everything about sisters is hunky-dory. Of course, we've had our share of scraps and disagreements. Sisters can sometimes take advantage of the kinship bond to get away with something they would never do to a friend. Also, sisters don't always tell you what they really think about you; they tell each other, but not you. In our family, there's a great deal of that.

Growing up in our large family, perfection was the rule, and mistakes and shortcomings were not tolerated. We still find it difficult to admit guilt, and words of apology don't come easily. But the best part about sisters is that the hostility is quickly dissolved as soon as we choose to let it go. Eventually, a pressing need or some act of kindness will intercede to override the offense and restore the loving relationship.

I haven't always appreciated sisters or living in a large family. I'm basically a solitary individual. I felt as though there were always too many people around. Also, I was known as the Goody Two-Shoes of the family. I always did the right thing and never had to be disciplined. But I learned the value of sibling loyalty one summer Sunday when I was eight years old.

Dad was working one of his many weekend jobs and Mom elected not to attend church service. The children piled into Granddad's Buick and headed to the Mount Zion Baptist Church. Granddad was a trustee, so we were prepared to spend the better part of the afternoon in church. It must have been older brother Richard's bright idea to skip service and visit Aunt Lena and Uncle Mack, who lived a short walk from the church. Richard was somewhat a miscreant. Years later, as preteens, as we lined up for baptism in the small church in Harlem, New York, where Uncle Frank was pastor, it was Richard who convinced us that Uncle Frank was trying to drown us because we "must be born again."

Richard knew that if we left immediately after Sunday school, we could visit Aunt Lena an Uncle Mack and return to church by the time Granddad finished counting the offering, and Granddad would be none the wiser. Being childless, Aunt Lena and Uncle Mack welcomed a house full of kids and lavished us with fruit, candy, and a dime apiece. Aunt Lena allowed us to play with her prized porcelain doll collection that adorned the top of her china closet. Uncle Mack entertained the boys with small talk on the front porch.

The scheme would have gone off without a hitch, except I had an attack of guilt. Arriving home, I felt it was my moral obligation to inform Mom and Dad of the crime we had committed. As punishment, the others were sent upstairs to spend the remainder of the afternoon in their rooms. Although Mom had prepared a wonderful Sunday dinner of ham, green beans, and potato salad, Dad opened two cans of cold pork and beans and delivered them upstairs with a spoon for each person. He said he wanted them to experience what it was like to be in prison. I, on the other hand, dined elegantly at the dining room table. But it was the loneliest dinner I had ever had, my punishment for being a snitch. That day I learned a lesson in sibling loyalty that I have never forgotten.

Mom may have purposely created such solidarity. Now as adults, we live separate lives in clusters within disparate locations. I was first to separate from the family. Upon completion of graduate school, I remained in Washington, DC. Carol was next to relocate with me, as I persuaded her that she could make a more significant contribution living in the nation's capital. Gradually, others were to follow. Similarly, when Millie decided to retire from the airline industry and relocate to the suburbs of Atlanta, Midge followed.

While Mom and Dad were with us, no one missed a holiday gathering at the family homestead. We filled a room with the Christmas tree and gifts from each person to all the others and had indoor snowball fights from the mounds of wrapping paper. Now at Thanksgiving, all who are able travel for four days of family fun and a sumptuous gourmet meal at Millie's mansion in Georgia. At some point a party breaks out. Family reunions are held biannually at some exotic location. During the year, we gather together on Christmas Eve, and save Christmas for smaller intimate dinners at each separate home.

Throughout our lives, I've never had a personal dispute with Carol. We are close in age and have similar world perspectives. We talk for hours, sharing experiences, thoughts, and opinions. When I was fifteen, it was Carol who dictated the college I would attend. The day before my college graduation, as I sat on the steps of the residence house lonely for company, I had never been so delighted as when I saw her beige Volkswagen Beetle rounding the corner as if Carol seemed to sense that I needed her. In times when Carol's views and practices differ from mine, a deep bond still binds us in spirit.

Carol is undoubtedly the glue that holds our family together. Her absence from a family gathering leaves a noticeable void. While I would have donated a kidney to any of my siblings, it was special to donate to Carol because of her importance to the family. That made the transplant a family affair because everyone was emotionally and spiritually invested. I had no doubt I would be a perfect match as a kidney donor and that Anastasia would find a perfectly matched physical and spiritual host. We've had our differences, but my sisters and brothers have always been there for me through thick or thin, and I for them.

Self-Determination

In the black church, a woman never married and childless is an oddity, regarded with either suspicion or pity. For some reason, married people believe they are the sole standard for a righteous life. I had not felt myself to be a peculiarity until one afternoon on an extended trip to Russia shortly after the demise of the former Soviet Union. I was intrigued by life behind the Iron Curtain since my only exposure was through faulty images from Hollywood, particularly Boris and Natasha in the now ancient cartoon series *The Rocky and Bullwinkle Show*.

Since Russian launched the first satellite, most Americans feared the country, believing it had the competitive edge in technology, as well as its finger on the button of the atomic bomb. Russians were similarly interested in American ways. So it was a special treat in St. Petersburg, as I was invited to tea at the humble home of a young divorced mom and her college-age daughter.

As she served tea on the luggage trunk that served as a coffee table in their sparsely furnished living room, which doubled as a bedroom, the mother posed the question of why American women don't marry. Russians held as many stereotypes of us as we did of them. This was the first time I was called upon to justify my being.

In formulating a cogent response, I drew upon the memory of a youthful era. I clearly recalled the singular moment some time in my second decade when I decided not to bring children into this chaotic world. So a single lifestyle was the chosen path. I had considered marriage in a previous relationship but realized that I had not developed into who I am. I did not have the right emotional tools and most of all, I was not cut out for the role of Stepford wife. As for financial security, I desired to put my own mettle to the test.

Throughout the years, I have had role models for successful single living, and no pressure from Mom or Dad. Dad's favorite Aunt Lillian never married her beloved while they lived happily apart, albeit loyal and committed. It was Aunt Lillian who served as a model for a loving aunt, as Myke and I spent numerous adolescent summers under her watchful care down South. In keeping with her tradition, I take the role of aunt very seriously. I've put braces on teeth, paid tuition, and even cosigned a loan or two. It is my special tradition to deck the little girls in formal attire and escort them to *The Nutcracker* ballet each Christmas.

Moreover, on the subject of marriage, one of Mom's favorite admonishments was "If you know like I know, you'll never get married." Mom never had the opportunity to accomplish her dreams so she helped her children accomplish theirs, and for this we are grateful for her sacrifice. I'm not sure I know what Mom knew, but what I do know is over the years, I've done alright. I lack nothing I desire. I'm not lonely and I have dozens of nieces and nephews to spoil. I have a secure future, I have complete autonomy over my life, I am free to make my own decisions and I love my independence. So when it came to the revelation to become a kidney donor, I had no pressures to the contrary.

In regard to organ donation, sometimes others impose their will upon the potential donor and in so doing, thwart the will of God. It may be a spouse, sibling, child, or other relation. They convince us that we're taking too much risk or are too old, too young, or not healthy enough; speculate about what if; and so on. In actuality, it is their own fear. When this occurs, it is important to recognize your personal relationship with God and trust God's command, obey and know that before anyone is called to a divine action, God has already equipped you with whatever is necessary to accomplish the task.

Transformation

In the New Testament, transformation is associated with a renewal of the mind. In the general sense, spiritual transformation refers to a reversal of consciousness, usually a conversion from sinful ways to righteousness. In our family, the transformation inspired by the transplant was spiritual maturity, increase in the depth of our faith, enhancement of our prayer life, and appreciation for the family as a divine institution.

In the months following the surgery, Carol and I traded thoughts and memories of the experience. Carol is always one to provide philosophical interpretation. Our discussions were filled with ruminations about the changes observed in the family and in our lives. We kept each other abreast of our healing process and the changes as they occurred. We reminisced about our upbringing and the specific incidents that shaped who we became and culminated with the transplant. It became evident that there was much to share with the world that could inform and enrich the lives of others. Donating Anastasia was not the end of my journey. The final installment in fulfillment of the divine revelation is the production of this book.

In the aftermath of the transplant, people have asked whether there is a special connection between Carol and me. They expect to hear a tale of the supernatural such as a mysterious ability to sense each other's thoughts and desires, or that Carol has assumed one of my characteristics. Although we are profoundly altered by the experience emotionally and spiritually, we have experienced nothing supernatural. Certainly there was and will always be an emotional bond between us. But it is one we created based in joy derived from the giving, and the response of eternal gratitude. For us, this emotional bond is unique. Indeed, for most transplants, the recipient and donor are not related and the donor's identity is not revealed to the recipient.

Eventually, because of continual cell replacement, there will come a time when Anastasia's cells will be replaced by those created in Carol's body, and all cells from me will be extinguished. Hence physically, Anastasia will not be mine. She will belong solely to Carol. But spiritually, Carol will permanently own a piece of my soul, and the bond between Carol and me will last to eternity. It is a bond crafted from unique capacities that define what it means to be a spiritually transformed human.

In the summer following the transplant the entire family came together for its biannual reunion for four days in Myrtle Beach, South Carolina. It was a rare occasion for each of the siblings to be present at a family event. We gathered from regions of the country including Kansas, Georgia, Missouri, New York, Maryland, Virginia, and Washington, DC. In the past, the entire family had gathered only to bid farewell to Mom, Dad, our brother Richard, and niece Courtney. The reunion served as a wakening call and stimulated each of us to appreciate the delicate bond between family members and how easily any one of us could be lost. We realized that these moments together were precious, and it is far better to come together for a joyous occasion than at the passing of a loved one.

A family tradition, we bestowed gifts of recognition and appreciation for feats of accomplishment and honor. Indeed the transplant had been the most important incident in recent history. Therefore Millie and Midge were presented with engraved silver boxes. For Marvin, Cony, Marcella, and Charlotte, there were embossed silver and crystal mementos for their caregiving efforts. For me, Carol composed a plaque with her heartfelt sentiments (below). To the delight of all, we announced the intention to produce a book.

This final chapter was the most difficult to write. After a full year in preparing the manuscript, I sensed that the culminating event that would signify the family's transformation had yet to be accomplished. I fretted that perhaps tragedy loomed on the horizon. Maybe Anastasia would be rejected after all.

MESSAGE OF GRATITUDE TO KAY
For the Precious Healing Gift
of a Kidney

Beloved One,

Mere words could never express the depth of gratitude in my heart for your gift of your kidney we named Anastasia. The Christ in you has raised the quality of life for me both physically and spiritually. As a loving and courageous donor, you graciously prepared to release a healthy organ to me. You shared a part of yourself and I joyously received. I AM certain we were born to do this, in order to learn that in God, giving is receiving. As I received love from every family member, I came to understand that we do not heal alone. All who love are invested in the one who travels the healing path. Therefore Anastasia belongs to all of us. I AM so happy to receive her cell memory because I admire you greatly in all your selfless giving. I often tease that I have finally earned my Ph.D. (Praise for Help Delivered). You have genuinely supported me in every victory and valley of my recovery. I AM happy to help fulfill your dream of sharing the "coincidences" that indicate divine order in this experience so that so others may donate for transplants. I vow to ever cherish the gift. Thank you. Bless you, in Christ's light and love.

Your sister,
Carol

As I sat before the laptop mulling these words, the blare of the telephone disrupted my concentration. Something about its sudden nature and intensity led me to expect an urgent matter. My niece Naomi had been admitted to Johns Hopkins Hospital. Barely a dozen years on this earth, Naomi's spindly body for the past two weeks raged a fierce battle with a condition resistant to cure. Formerly a straight-A student, she had missed many days of school, which caused her grades to plummet to B's and C's.

By the time word spread through the family, the report of "leukopenia" had been mislabeled as "leukemia." *Leukopenia* is medical terminology for a low white blood cell count. In actuality, it is the opposite of leukemia, which is characterized by a high quantity of abnormal white blood cells. The airwaves and cyberspace were alight with speculative chatter as family members sprang into conversation awaiting a report of the diagnosis. Was there another transplant on the horizon? If Naomi required a bone marrow transplant, who would be the likely donor?

A triumphant transforming effect was evidenced in the family's response. For African American bone marrow donors, the odds of being a suitable match are very low; and there exists a common myth that donation involves a painful procedure. Nonetheless, not one but *every* eligible adult willingly stepped up to the plate and volunteered to be tested. I, too, would have gladly thrown my hat in the ring. I had signed up on bethematch.org years earlier in a donor drive at church.

Praises to God, Naomi's condition was cured through intravenous antibiotics, and she is once again a healthy adolescent. But the transplant experience left an indelible imprint on our family as well as a sensitivity to health needs and our role in supporting one another. Some have confided that since the transplant, in renewing their driver's license, they acquired a donor card. I am certain that in case of any tragic loss, the family members will consent to organ donation. In light of our heightened awareness and sensitivity, it is difficult to imagine that, if called upon, someone would refuse to donate. Confidence in this is exhibited in our prayer life.

I am witness to the spiritual maturation of our family. During prayer sessions, we recite the Lord's Prayer and read aloud the written requests of each family member. Each person then offers a powerful personal prayer. In the past, these requests have been for material outcomes. Presently, our prayers have become praises of thanksgiving for blessings, intercessory prayers, and petitions for the state of the country and the world.

We seek to align our requests with God's will for humankind. We ask to be strengthened in order to assume our role in effecting the outcome. Thus, we pray not for things but situations; not for self but for humankind. We no longer beseech God for our wishes but invite God into our lives so God's will can be manifested through us and our deeds. We end in firm belief with the affirmation, "And so it is."

No doubt, we have not always been in agreement. For example, in yesteryears we spent far too much money on meaningless Christmas gifts. Some people had to open a savings account and contribute all year long in order to avoid going into debt. We came to realize that we already possessed too many material things and did not need another tie, pen, scarf, or blender. Carol suggested we pool our funds and make a sizable donation to charity. She found an organization that supplies farm animals to rural residents in developing countries. Remembering the Chinese proverb "Give a man a fish and you feed him for a day. Teach a man to fish and you feed him for a lifetime," we were excited to do our part for an anonymous struggling family.

That Christmas was a turning point in family history. Indeed, the gift to charity led to appreciation of the true meaning of the season and understanding of what giving is about. I wish I could report that we made this a family tradition. In a family the size of ours, of course, some members opposed. As a group, we have never given to charity again. But each year at Christmas, I do not spend hours in crowded malls shopping for items that will be used once then placed on the shelf. Instead, in my family's name, I donate to my favorite charity, the Washington Area Food Bank. There is an occasional Christmas gift from someone's heart. For example, Charlotte is fond of knitting and crocheting lovely crafts that are always adored and appreciated.

Today, the family continues to evolve as an institution. This is not by plan or design; rather it evolves as individuals take interest in a particular project. This year, we collaborated on a unique Mother's Day project compiling Mom's colorful sayings into a volume titled *Momma Said*. We reminisce and laugh about the admonishments we received growing up such as, "Too bad you're not too old for your wants to hurt you." Mom's influence on our lives will now be passed to future generations. We will construct a quilt depicting our family tree, which will be held by the elder member of each generation and passed down accordingly to each successive generation.

We are incorporated as Family Matrix, LLC, a not-for profit organization. Myke, who always wanted to be an artist, designed a family crest. Adoption of a crest is an ancient tradition in which group members adorn an emblem that represents the virtues they uphold. The tradition of the family crest is traced to the royal families of medieval times. Our family crest is affixed to our prayer list so that we may recognize its meaning and meditate upon it during prayer sessions. The crest displays a turtle ascending inside a three-pronged border of emerald green. The triangular frame symbolizes the Holy Trinity. The green hue represents health, wealth, and oneness with nature. The turtle progresses upward, mindfully and with determination, free from hasty decisions and actions.

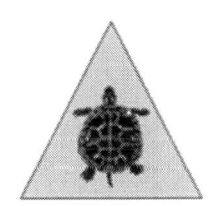

Midge has become the family historian. She traces our African American family heritage and genealogy through records of deceased relatives. She discovered a family tradition in which individuals were assigned the names of our forebears. Most of our ancestors were listed in the census as mulattoes. Granddad on Mom's side was two generations removed from slavery. Born of a free man, Granddad's father, whose wife was Native American, plus several siblings were schoolteachers. According to oral history, Dad's great-grandfather, who was said to be Native American, fought in the Civil War and retired on his war injuries until the day he encountered a snake and jumped up from his wheelchair and ran!

We adopted a family credo. It is necessary to write down family values for present and future generations as a means of sustaining family identity and unity. Our family credo (below) is patterned after the Baptist Church Covenant. It is always a beautiful occasion at church when on communion Sunday the congregation recites the church covenant in unison. It is not only a pledge for righteous conduct but a unifying force for the body of Christ. We were happy to adopt this tradition in our family. The family credo adorns the walls of each family member's home and we recite it together at prayer sessions. These are a few of the things that make our family an institution of divine order.

We're not perfect people for certain. This book only presents the good stuff. Rather, we are being perfected, that is, fulfilling the purpose for which we were endowed with life. A mechanism of ensuring right behavior we practice is intervention. An intervention is a direct group confrontation with someone who has gone astray conducted in a loving atmosphere. No one wants to be the focus of a family intervention. One Thanksgiving I voiced my intention to try out the browning feature of my new microwave oven on the turkey. Family members took a poll and voted to instruct me not to do it. Today more serious intervention takes place by social media. Imagine the effect of being bombarded with random positive messages of love and encouragement. Social media is also a great way to mend a broken relationship when words of apology are hard to muster. Some of the more common texts include: ILY (I love you), SRY (sorry), IMS (I'm sorry), LY (love you), and XOXOXO (hugs and kisses). We try never to forget to say "I love you" when we hang up the phone.

On several occasions, I have been invited to speak about the transplant experience. Audiences are fascinated by the events that led to the revelation as well as the transformative effects on our family. Often posed is the question of whether the sale of organs should be legal. My response is a resounding, "Blasphemy!" Organs are not our possessions to sell. We are merely stewards of what God has entrusted to us to achieve God's purpose. Transformation is God's reward when an organ is willingly and freely given to another in love and obedience. In so doing, the symbol of the cross is effectuated in the

Family Credo

Inspired by the Holy Spirit as Believers in our risen Savior and Lord, and baptized in the name of the Father, Son and Holy Ghost, we do now in the presence of God, the Heavenly host, the spirit essence of our forebears, and each to the other, enter into this covenant and solemnly pledge to uphold its premises.

We engage therefore through prayerful reverence with the aid of God and family to coexist in harmony and Christian fellowship; to strive for the advancement of each other, family, and African American people for knowledge, holiness, prosperity and justice; to promote unity through constant prayer and worship; to keep ourselves virtuous and morally upright; maintain Christian faith and values; sustain dignity through righteousness, cleanliness, discipline and respect for self and others; and to be zealous in our efforts to seek these things when they are lacking.

We also engage to be forthright and truthful in our dealings, faithful in engagements and exemplary in comportment; to abstain from gossip, profane language, excessive anger and any unlawful or violent acts; as well as the sale and use of harmful or addictive substances; to be slow to take offense and always ready to be forgiving and to secure forgiveness from others without delay.

We further engage to watch over one another in selfless love, to sacrifice comfort, time and resources to aid those in despair; to promote physical, emotional and spiritual well-being; to educate, baptize and religiously instruct our children; to continually participate in the exercise of democratic government and to be ever willing to serve and defend human rights.

We moreover engage to maintain a continual affiliation with a church where we can financially support its ministries, spread the gospel and seek salvation for ourselves, our kindred and acquaintances as we carry forth the spirit of this covenant and the principles of God's Word.

intersection of the horizontal pole which represents the love manifested between humans, with the vertical pole which symbolizes connection with God above. Thus, organ *donation* is divine. I will, however, go so far as to say that organ donation as a redeeming action might in some cases reconcile a broken relationship with God and the human community. Organ donation can be a vehicle for recompense and restitution. An exemplar is incarcerated individuals who are indebted to society.

My friend Jack was an elected official. An otherwise righteous person, Jack was lured by lust for money to commit an act for which he is now serving seven years. He is already forgiven of God, but organ donation can be an unselfish, humanitarian means to restore his dignity and self-esteem, as well as his relationship to society. In more serious cases, organ donation from a violent offender could be an even exchange for a life taken or disrupted.

Donating Anastasia affected my life in multiple ways, albeit with the exception of physical health. There have been no physical ramifications. Each change has had a positive and rippling effect. Organ donation is a venture not to be entered into lightly but with reverence, obedience, and humility. But once endeavored, it is an awesome transformative force.

As for my personal transformation, today I enjoy a deepened personal relationship with God, and day after day, the existence of God is proven. Whenever I am obedient to the revealed will of God in my life, I am fearless. In the summer following the transplant, I attended a retreat at a resort in the Shenandoah Mountains, a three-hour drive from Washington. On the return trip, the commercial bus engaged for our transport was caught in what could only have been a tornado. It was as if the bus were a miniature child's toy and someone was dousing its path with washtubs of ice water. The bus, bottom-heavy and light at the top, came dangerously close to being toppled on its side by the ferocious wind. Some passengers cried while others silently prayed. By convention, I had chosen the first passenger seat across from the driver. I sat attentively, with spirit serene, and assured in my soul that his was not to be my demise. The serenity and assurance surely affected the driver, as well as other passengers. I offered words of comfort to a passenger, assuring her that all was well because she was with me, and I am protected.

I have also undergone a change in my prayer life. At first I was concerned, since it seemed I had abandoned the long-held prayer and meditation ritual that I dedicated to God when I awakened each morning. This daily ritual was special, as it was my individual fellowship with God, and it set the tone for the day.

That was before the transformation. Currently, I do not need to set aside a separate time for prayer because I constantly walk in fellowship with God every second of the day.

I talk to God through every event and every situation I encounter. I listen for the still, small voice and look for signs of assurance. I never worry about making a wrong decision because I know my thoughts are aligned with God's will and my purpose for being. Of course I still pray, but it is not relegated to a religious ritual.

Scholars note that there is but a single figurative reference to organ transplant in the Bible. The prophet Ezekiel admonished the people to obtain a new heart and hence, a new spirit. Through my family and my experiences, I am witness to the transformative power of living kidney donation.

Epilogue

It was a warm Sunday in late spring, the second anniversary of the revelation that led me to become a kidney donor. The family gathered at home after church to enjoy a scrumptious meal and our monthly prayer session. I had recently returned from a thoroughly fascinating study tour of Cuba. A resolute nation frozen in time, Cuba led me to discover as much about myself, my comfortable lifestyle, and my capitalist mentality as I did about the Cubans.

Carol arrived cheery and energetic, bearing her monthly floral bouquet and transporting herself not with the usual wheeled walker but with two canes. Her mobility is improving daily. Carol continues to take her health seriously, keeps her appointments, and maintains her medicinal regimen. Decked in a dressy short-sleeve summer ensemble, she had cut her once draping locks into a classy, short bobbed style necessitated by the drying effect of the medications. Nevertheless, her foot blisters had healed and her skin was clear and smooth, no longer with the blotchy puffiness that marked the months of dialysis.

The family prayed in the manner that had become customary after the transplant and our spiritual transformation. Once they departed, I completed the arduous task of tidying up and later settled into the comfort of bed to surf the channels in search of an interesting informative program. Finding none, I snuggled beneath the cozy covers and dropped off into peaceful sleep.

Dr. Kay T. Payne is professor of communications at Howard University, a historically black university in Washington, DC. She grew up in a loving family of twelve children in Winston-Salem, N.C., who later migrated to New York City. She recently obtained a master's degree in religious studies focusing on theological bioethics. She has traveled worldwide and she delights audiences with amazing tales of her adventures. She is a highly sought-after speaker and lecturer. She loves yoga, fitness, and preparing gourmet meals for family.

"Spellbinding, inspiring, informative."

"A must-read for anyone who never considered organ donation."

"Over the top!"

"At times funny, serious, and spiritual."

Made in the USA
Lexington, KY
06 February 2016